QUIGLEY SELL YOUR HOME

THE ULTIMATE GUIDE TO ILLINOIS REAL ESTATE

RANDI LYNN QUIGLEY

BALBOA.PRESS

A DIVISION OF HAY HOUSE

Balboa Press books may be ordered through booksellers or by contacting:

Balboa Press
A Division of Hay House
1663 Liberty Drive
Bloomington, IN 47403
www.balboapress.com
844-682-1282

Because of the dynamic nature of the Internet, any web addresses or links contained in this book may have changed since publication and may no longer be valid. The views expressed in this work are solely those of the author and do not necessarily reflect the views of the publisher, and the publisher hereby disclaims any responsibility for them.

The author of this book does not dispense medical advice or prescribe the use of any technique as a form of treatment for physical, emotional, or medical problems without the advice of a physician, either directly or indirectly. The intent of the author is only to offer information of a general nature to help you in your quest for emotional and spiritual well-being. In the event you use any of the information in this book for yourself, which is your constitutional right, the author and the publisher assume no responsibility for your actions.

Any people depicted in stock imagery provided by Getty Images are models, and such images are being used for illustrative purposes only. Certain stock imagery © Getty Images.

Print information available on the last page.

ISBN: 978-1-9822-6627-1 (sc)
ISBN: 978-1-9822-6628-8 (e)

Balboa Press rev. date: 03/31/2021

CONTENTS

"To be successful in real estate, you must always and consistently put your clients' best interests first. When you do, your personal needs will be realized beyond your greatest expectations." – Randi Lynn

*Please Note that this book is written stating my personal opinion of how I perceive the Real Estate market from my Experience as a Full Time Professional Realtor in the South and Southwest Chicagoland Area – Randi Lynn

LIST

SELL

Close

REPEAT

Do THIS To Have Great Showings And Get "Top Dollar" For Your Home

*"Organizing is what you do before you do something,
so that when you do it, it is not all mixed up."*

When it comes to selling ANYTHING (not just real estate) it's the buyer that matters. Not the seller. So it is very important to make sure that your home is as appealing and neutral as it can be to all parties walking in viewing your home.

You should think of completely DECLUTTERING and organizing your home. I know many real estate agents out there are *thinking* it, but some are too timid to tell their clients this. I understand this can be very time consuming; however, when you are listing your home to move, you are going to have to organize and most likely get rid of the clutter anyways... so why not do it before you list your home. This truly will give you much better Feedback on Showings and help sell your home faster, for the top dollar. In the relationship that Sellers have with their agent, there needs to be honest communication from both parties in order to have the most successful transaction. I always say that this is a Team Sport so it is my job to be as open and honest with you from the start that I can be.

Organizing and decluttering your home allows the potential buyers to be able to see the entire space and they will be able to envision what it's like to actually live there. That is the main goal, to make your house appealing to others.

Let's get into specifics.

The fridge is just *one* area that we see "decorated" that shouldn't be. Trust me, being a mom of 4 I get it! I have such a hard time not displaying all of my children's artwork ALL over the house. But as for the refrigerator, especially, when you are aiming to sell your home, try to keep it clean- think "Like New."

Now that we are discussing the kitchen, if you have any small appliances sitting out, put them in a pantry. I know you use your toaster daily, as well as some other items, but if whatever it is doesn't look good in a photo… …..put it away.

And that goes for the rest of the "stuff" in your house that buyers don't care to see. Think of your home as one of those model homes sold by a housing developer. They are bare—the idea is to create the psychological impression on potential buyers that this could be THEIR home. That this IS their home.

It almost goes without saying that creating this impression is really difficult if your personal stuff is everywhere.

Have Nothing In
Your House That
You Do Not Know To
Be Useful, or
Believe To Be
Beautiful

-William Morris

Here's a quick list of stuff to hide/put away:

- Toaster, mixer, and other kitchen appliances
- Knick knacks
- Book collections
- Posters
- Anything on your fridge (photos, magnets, etc)
- Magazines on the coffee table
- Newspapers

As you can probably tell by reading this list, your house should to be BARE! Completely Organized. This can literally be worth thousands and thousands of dollars to you in the final sale price. I do not, however, suggest completely depersonalizing your home. Some agents will tell you to take down all family pictures. Of course, I do not suggest leaving photos all over the home without frames, cluttered, etc. Yet, a family photo or pictures of the children (as long as you're comfortable with leaving them up) makes the home appear more welcoming.

I actually have a great tip... when showing your home, leave an empty laundry basket near the front door. Before you have a showing, make sure that you pick up anything that is just laying around, whether it be on the floor or counter top... wherever it may be. If it looks like it doesn't belong, put it in the basket and bring it with you! If you have a few minutes, take out the vacuum and make the clean lines in the carpet- simple! Also, put an air freshener right by the front door so as soon as they walk into your home they smell something AMAZING... These simple, little things, can help make the showing that much better for the potential buyers!!

Real estate is just as much art as it is science. Part of the "art" side of selling a home is value perception. And the perceived value of your home is much higher when it's clean, decluttered, and simply organized.

Let's get into even more specifics....

Family photos, again,...touchy subject. It's OK to have a couple family photos out, but when your entire house looks like a family museum.........you should probably take a few photos down. Remember, we have to allow the potential buyer to be able to envision themselves living there. Sometimes when all they see are family photos of YOUR family, they may not be able to truly see the home as their own.

Oh, and collectible Knick knacks. Can't forget those...

It is okay to have your collection but please, again, try to make sure that it is organized in a way that the buyer can still see all of the potential in your home, and that it does not take away from the Beautiful interior characteristics that we are trying to showcase and enhance.

Another tip that I would like to give is to also try to organize your garage and basement. These two spaces shouldn't serve as a "catch all." I realize that you may be thinking that possibly these areas are unfinished or that buyers really don't care about them... but the truth is that they do.

I would suggest maybe renting a storage unit and anything that you haven't physically used for a year, put it in there.

Here's an example for you to relate to: I am at a potential client's home giving them a Free Market Analysis. I am pleasantly surprised at how hard the sellers have worked to get it ready to place on the market.

Then we go into the garage.

Is the floor dirt, or concrete, or what? I don't know because I can't see it. Let me stop you right here... Buyers want to be able to see the home in its entirety. If you are using your garage and/ or basement as a storage unit, I would highly recommend either moving these items to an actual unit or possibly even donating these items.

There are a lot of organizations out there that would be happy to take what you aren't using. Let them! Or drop it off at a Good Will or a Donation location, there are many out there. Heck, there is one right here in New Lenox right next to the Walmart on Laraway. All you need to do is drive up and they come to your car and get what you would like to donate and it goes to a GREAT CAUSE! Or in Tinley Park, there is Together We Cope right off of Oak Park Avenue. This location goes to families in need. Clothes, furniture, even food!! (Unopened and unused of course) It's an amazing place, but I will leave that for another book.

Clutter doesn't just apply to the house. *It also applies to outdoor spaces.* We'll get to that in the next chapter. Point is, in order to sell your home for the best dollar with the least amount of market time, take some time and make it a priority. The cleaner, more organized, less cluttered your home is, the more buyers you will attract that can actually even result in multiple bids and a higher contract price that you have it listed for. (I have had this happen numerous times) We need to create a sense of urgency for the new buyers. The less they see, the quicker they feel they can make your home their own. We want to put in them a fear of loss, making them excited to write an immediate offer on your home upon leaving the showing.

This is your home. The more love and care you put into it, especially when listing it, the faster it will attract its new owners. The Buyers will be able to truly connect to your home, and it will leave a good, lasting, impression.

HOME

IS WHERE YOUR STORY BEGINS.

I want to help you start your story.

You Only Get One Chance To Make A First Impression: The Absolute Importance of CURB APPEAL

"Never forget that you only have one opportunity to make a first impression- with Buyers, with Marketing, with Everything You Do"

You've probably heard the expression "curb appeal" before. It's not some secret marketing strategy used by realtors. Everybody knows about curb appeal. But most people do NOT realize just *how* important it actually is.

Advertising gurus say that the headline is the most important part of the ad. Why? Because if the headline doesn't grab your attention, you won't read the rest! You have to get people to read the headline first. Real estate is no different.

Your curb appeal is your "headline."

You are selling not just your house, but the land it sits on also. If you think cleaning out your garage means "place it alongside the house," think again.

Pulling up to a house that has either a car collection in the driveway, old couches or other old furniture stacked up behind it, or basically anything that wouldn't typically be there when looking at "New Construction" (*with of course the exception of landscaping*) greatly takes away from the curb appeal. Trust me on this one.

Here is an example that I'm sure we all can relate to: I'm showing a house in late May, where beautiful flowers are starting to bloom and it is literally a lovely time of year, but the bright orange pumpkin lawn and leaf bags still adorn the house as if those bags are an artful piece of landscaping…

Not so much.

Halloween was seven months ago. Please, just spend ten minutes cleaning up the yard to boost the curb appeal. This could mean thousands of dollars in the final sales price, because it directly affects the *emotionally-driven* **perceived value.** I'm not saying that you all *have to* put fresh flowers out or anything of that sort. (*Though it may actually help*) Again, trust me on this one… I actually suggest buying some Gorgeous Silk outdoor flowers. I had a habit of forgetting to water my plants and literally I ended up being the neighbor who displayed half lively plants outside, until one day actually my Grandma noticed and brought over some silk "fake" flowers for me. Haha. They look real! No one even knows the difference. But simple touches on the outside make the home that more inviting on the inside.

Fill A House
With LOVE
And It Becomes
A Home

Point being, if your home is not in season with the outdoor décor. I would highly suggest taking a few minutes and put some love and attention to the outside as well.

Remember, most people start their home search on the Internet. If your house is not appealing *outside*, chances are they won't go *inside*. It's like going fishing without bait….you probably won't catch much fish.

Another thing to remember on the outside is the *not-so-pleasant* subject of pet waste. Some surprises are good, but when you step in a steamy pile of dog *waste* on a hot summer day, it's not so good. If a buyer has to walk through your yard with their head down trying to avoid stepping into *anything*, what you are actually doing is taking away from that buyer's full experience. These buyers are now focusing on something other than the exterior qualities and potential of your home.

When it comes to cleaning and/or organizing, **put it on the top of your priority list.** If you don't have time, get less sleep… It's really that important.

If you can't do that, either hire it out, or bribe a friend. I have found that if I ask a friend, not only can it be enjoyable for you both, but you can exchange time and help them with a project at their house later on. Win-win.

Let me ask you this: **if you are in the market for a new car,** how impressed would you be if there were empty fast food bags, containers of half eaten fries, gum wrappers, and some dirty laundry inside? Car dealers would NEVER put a car on the for sale lot until it was completely clean and detailed. They often pay professional cleaners to make sure it's spotless!

It's standard in the car industry to make sure the product is clean. And, well, it's standard in **pretty much every other industry, too.** When was the last time you went to the mall and there was garbage in a retail store?

When we buy stuff, we expect it to be clean. It's not a nice extra, or a bonus. It's the price of entry. It's *expected.*

Here's what I'm getting at: People are SHOPPING when they tour your home! If retail stores maintain an immaculate level of cleanliness to sell $30 shirts, shouldn't you present your home with an equal attention to detail? After all, most homes are a few hundred thousand dollars. Or more! Again, when we look at things from a different perspective such as this, they may become easier to relate to. That is my main goal here in writing this chapter.

When you stop and think about it, it's crazy that anyone would buy a home that wasn't absolutely spotless. I would go as far as to recommend hiring professional cleaners if you *really* want your home to sell quickly. It *does* make a difference in how well your home "shows."

And while we're on the topic of cleaning, can I talk about another unpleasantly? *Again, I am just being honest.*

Odor.

It may seem strange, but many people put a name on each house they see, to help them remember it. And it usually has to do with the smells.

I remember showing the hamster house, the cat house, the candle house, the cookie house, and the famous GARBAGE HOUSE ... to name a few.

The "garbage house" was, from the outside, a storybook house. It was like the Hansel and Gretel house. Just beautiful! You almost expected gingerbread cookies to be baking when you walked in. But when I opened the door, the buyers RAN back to the car! (*Almost literally*)

When it comes to human memory, guess which of the five senses is strongest? Yep---smell!

Scientists have documented that smells send powerful signals to the memory center of our brain, the hypothalamus. In fact, the olfactory system (fancy word for "sense of smell") is part of the brain's *limbic system*. The limbic system is responsible for memories and emotions.

When you smell a new scent for the first time, you link it to an event, a person, a thing, or even a moment. Your brain forges a link between the smell and a memory -- associating the smell of chlorine with summers at the pool or hot dogs with baseball games, etc.

When you encounter the smell again, *the link is already there*, ready to evoke a memory or a mood.

What does this mean for you as a home seller? People will REMEMBER what your house smells like. Because of its location in the brain's limbic system, smell evokes strong *memories* and *emotions*.

If you're trying to sell your home for top dollar, even the slightest unpleasant odors can potentially ruin a potential sale, unfortunately.

So there's what NOT to do. But here's something you've probably heard before that you *should* do. And if you haven't already, here it is:

<u>A little paint goes a LONG way!</u>

Fresh Paint
Will Allow
The Potential
New Buyer
The Ability To
See Your Home
As A Blank Canvas

-Randi Lynn

Fresh, neutral paint is the most inexpensive way to boost the value of your home. Period.

You may think your little child's finger painting is cute on the wall, but the buyers will beg to differ. When a home is marketed as "Freshly Painted," it almost gives the perception to buyers as "Move-In-Ready."

Over time, you have probably changed your artwork around, moved furniture around, and maybe (probably) accumulated some scratches or other "wall injuries."

Let me tell you a basic rule of thumb...

If you drive around your city, look on the internet, or get ideas from Pinterest, *and don't see anything remotely close to what you're thinking of for a paint scheme*, don't do it.

Different is fine *if you are staying in your home.* Go for it.

If you're selling, it is not the time for daring or to be different. If you have old awnings, remove them. Old faded shutters - either paint them, or remove them. Sometimes it's as simple as getting out the pressure washer.

Spiders, dirt, and general uncleanliness can make your house look neglected. Remember: your home should be SPOTLESS before selling. Not "clean" in a general sense, but *spotless.* You know, able to pass a "white glove test." *(Or at least as clean as you can get it. I do understand that all of this does take time, in which it seems passes by all too quickly at times)*

17

I'll again return to the car metaphor: your home should be as clean as a brand new car. Even if it was built in the 1940's, it should at least *feel* like a new home.

It's a PRODUCT and you are displaying it!

You've probably heard the quote, "It's the little things." What we have discussed so far has not been expensive big-ticket items, but maintenance items. It all matters!

I know, I know......... Sometimes it's hard to objectively look at your home from the perspective of a buyer, *but that is exactly what you need to do.* And this is why many listings sit on the market for months and months, sometimes even having a birthday.

Newsflash: your home should not have a "for sale" birthday. If it's been on the market for an entire year, it's time for a change!

In general, a home should never take more than 90 days to sell in a hot Spring Market. If it hasn't had multiple showings, inquiries, and offers before that time in a very active market, something is wrong (usually this means it's overpriced, but there can be a variety of factors at play). *Adequately pricing your home will be discussed later in this book.*

Again, this is *general* advice. In some markets and neighborhoods, demand is simply lower, and a house might sit for 150 days. It all depends on supply and demand, and how long you are comfortable waiting. Or how long you can *afford* to wait for your home to sell.

What many sellers don't realize is the more DOM a home racks up (agent lingo for "days on market"), the more its reputation begins to suffer. Most buyers will become suspicious if a home has been on the market for a long time. They'll subconsciously think something is horribly wrong with it, or that the home is extremely overpriced (even if it is only *slightly* overpriced). Don't let this happen to you!

That's when you need an **honest** agent (or a trusted friend) to walk through your home as if they were purchasing it.

When they pull into the driveway, does it look inviting? Is the grass armpit high? Do you have weeds growing in your yard or in between sidewalks? Is your trash bin overflowing in the driveway? Upon walking in the door, do you smell a nice scented candle? Or do you smell a cat box? Maybe walk around the exterior of your house and prune trees in walkways, or those that are leaning against the house... it is the attention to little details that go such a LONG WAY in Real Estate.

I have shown properties where bathrooms have not been checked... try to remember to flush your toilets. Pay attention to the small little details of your daily life while living in your home. Be aware of the surroundings, and that will make all the difference.

Another thing I can't stress enough is *valuables*. PLEASE, for your sake and the sake of the agent showing, put them away.

And that brings me to another important issue: make sure the agent showing your house has actually "qualified" their buyers. There are so many times I have worked with other agents who tell me an offer is coming in, then to find out that the buyer cannot even purchase the home. It's unfortunate.

How does that make you feel about selling yourself as a "for sale by owner?" I'm not trying to scare you. But you do need to be aware of potential risks of selling your home by owner and be aware of things that can happen along the way to prevent you from selling your home.

And speaking of doing things yourself, if you're not qualified... ... *I wouldn't recommend it*. When you are working with a licensed Real Estate Agent, it is our job to make sure the buyers we represent are legit, qualified buyers. This is a VERY BIG DEAL for many reasons for all involved in this process.

When prequalifying a buyer, it gives the buyer a price range to which they are qualified to purchase a home. This saves so much time and emotions, too, actually.

For an example, let's say this Gorgeous home comes up on the market that a buyer wants to see. They haven't yet talked to a lender but make pretty good money and believe they have a great credit score....

The home is listed at $375,000 and the buyers make an appointment to see the home. The agent at the time does not ask for a letter of preapproval or pre-qualification and shows the home. The buyer falls in love and wishes to place an offer. The next step is for them to talk with a lender to be able to get that original letter that I, as a Realtor, always need before showing my buyers any properties.

After speaking with the lender, the buyers are heartbroken to find out that they have only been pre-qualified to purchase up to $250,000. From this point on now the buyer is comparing every home they see with the first one, in which is listed at $125,000 over what they can afford. I'm sure you can see how this can be a huge problem. This is why talking to a lender should actually be a buyer's first step within the Real Estate Process. Any good realtor should advise their clients of this as well.

Whether or not the Realtor has provided feedback stating a potential offer may be made; This can be very disheartening for that seller who wants dearly to sell their home thinking an offer is coming in, only to find out that the buyer actually cannot afford your home that you just opened up for them to view.

Point is, when working with a Good Realtor, they will make sure that the buyers they personally show are qualified to purchase the homes they are setting up showings for. There are so many little details that need to be done in order to make a Real Estate Transaction Successful, and for the deal to actually close.

Licensed to

Sell

3

The Twelve Most Costly Mistakes Made By Homebuyers (And How To Avoid Them!)

1. Lack of Vision

A s Mark Twain said, "You cannot depend on your eyes when your imagination is out of focus."

This is so true! The average buyers have such difficulties seeing the potential in many of the homes that we see on showings…Because of that, I absolutely *love* working with buyers that have the rare gift of "vision." The majority of people simply do not have it.

When I first started in real estate, I took this for granted. I just assumed my clients had the same "vision" I had for properties. You know, the ability to walk in to an outdated home… …and instead see it for what it *could* be. What it *should* be.

Have you ever watched one of those reality TV shows about home renovations? "Property Brothers" on *HGTV* is one of my favorites. The basic idea of every episode is two brothers (one's a contractor, one's a Realtor) attempt to convince someone to buy a "fixer upper," and spend the difference on an extensive renovation budget.

For example, instead of buying a $200,000 house, you purchase an ugly, outdated home that needs lots of repairs for $140,000.......... then spend the "extra" $60,000 renovating it into your absolute dream home.

Usually what happens is the buyer does not believe them. The property brothers try to convince the buyer that this *is* their dream home.....it just needs some work. The buyer is skeptical that a house "this ugly" could ever be modernized into a contemporary, updated home. In short, **they have no vision.**

Obviously, what happens is the "property brothers" and their crew renovate the ugly house into a BEAUTIFUL, updated home. Their vision allows them to see potential in ugly houses. And that's the big idea here. The key word is POTENTIAL.

Sure, there are plenty of properties out there that are just plain outdated and very unattrative. There's no other way of saying it. And you know exactly what I'm talking about! Outdated carpets, kitchens, bathrooms, paint.....you name it. I've seen it all.

Orland Park, for example, has plenty of "outdated" homes. For the most part, all of the new construction in Orland has been higher end homes in the mid $300,000 and up. Exceptions merely prove the rule. So the area has been pretty well established. Meaning, homes that have been around for a while are in need of much updating...

This means that for the "average" person who's looking to buy a $300,000 home in Orland Park, **there are lots and lots of**

opportunities to find bargain properties. Instead of buying a $300,000 home that's "move in ready," consider buying a $240,000 home that's cosmetically unattractive and needs some repairs. Invest the difference in a custom renovation that will turn a bargain "fixer upper" into your contemporary dream home.

Remember: cosmetic problems are usually the easiest and most affordable fixes. Older kitchen cabinets, appliances, carpets, and paint are not terribly expensive to replace. In fact, you'd be shocked at how far $10,000 can go!

In many cases, you can *completely transform* a home with as little as $10,000 of cosmetic upgrades.

Using the above example of buying an ugly $240,000 property instead of a "move in ready" house that's $300,000... ...think of what you could do with a $60,000 renovation budget!

This gives you a massive advantage as a house hunter. It means you can research many more homes than the average buyer, because you aren't confining your search to the relatively few homes that are truly "move in ready."

This World Is
But A Canvas
To Our Imagination

When you have vision, you have more options. And when you have more options, you have leverage during negotiations. And that's a very, very good thing!

And, besides, being "move in ready" is pretty subjective. Everybody has a different taste in interior design, layout, etc. Even on a home you originally think is perfect, you'll most likely change things.

Most of these ugly properties are usually passed by because buyers are so obsessed with homes that are "move in ready." As you know, homes that are really, truly, *move in ready* almost always have a premium price.

What this means for you is that if you have the patience and creativity to see the POTENTIAL in a home, you can score a major deal! Most buyers aren't willing to look at old, outdated homes. And if they are, they immediately want to move on to the next one!

It never even occurs to them that they could purchase an outdated/ugly home at a steep discount, and have plenty of money left over to completely renovate it into their dream home.

The vast, vast majority of house hunters only see the product that's there *right now.* They see the old carpets, the old paint, the outdated kitchen appliances, the poorly maintained yard. **People with vision see none of this; they see *opportunity*.**

2. Ignoring The *One Thing* You Cannot Change About A House

Rather than being concerned with cosmetics, here's the one thing you should *not* compromise on: location.

The old saying, "location, location, location" should be your top priority. It's a cliché for a reason!

Why? <u>Location is the one thing you can't change.</u>

This is a pretty profound insight: you can change ANYTHING about a house....*except location.* So when you find the perfect house in the perfect location, remember that anything and everything you don't like about it can be remedied!

Let me explain further....

I was working with a young couple, who I will call "Erin" and "Jon" (not their real names). They both came from upper middle class families. They were used to nice homes, newer cars, and all around being "comfy."

They wanted to buy their first house on their own, together. Their budget was *not* going to get them a newer house in an upscale neighborhood.

They needed to compromise.

I made some calls and set up tours at a few local properties with larger yards, which they had requested. Because they needed space and were on a lower budget, the homes that we viewed, well, tended to need a little imagination!

With some elbow grease, some rearranging of walls and a little money, some of these would have been close to perfect! The square footage was also what they were asking for.

But Erin and Jon lacked VISION.

They insisted on looking at houses that were "pretty," with very small yards and not much square footage. The house they chose *was* pretty. BUT....none of the homes around it were! They were "The Big Fish in the Little Pond."

Erin and Jon broke one of the cardinal rules of real estate: it's always better to own the most unimproved house in a neighborhood than the most over improved house in a neighborhood.

About six months later, when they were starting a family, they realized they already needed to move! To make matters worse, they took a loss on the house when they eventually sold it. Not good.

The previous owners had already made all the improvements, and, for the size, the house had met its maximum value for quite some time. Every home reaches a certain point where it doesn't matter how many upgrades it has—it simply cannot sell for more than X amount of dollars.

Against my counsel, Erin and Jon bought a house that wasn't right for them. It's important for me to point out that the house they purchased wasn't intrinsically a bad house.....it was just a bad house *for them*. See the difference?

Now, there is a happy ending to this story. They DID listen the 2nd time around. We found a house that was clearly in need of much updating and renovations. It was not the most attractive....

BUT....the yard was perfect and the location was perfect for their job commutes. We went through the house with an open mind and came up with a renovation plan. They took down walls to open up the floorplan, added some nice fixtures, flooring, and really opened up the place. With some exterior renovating to put the icing on the cake, the house went from the ugly toad to the handsome prince!

3. Failure To Research and Interview *Multiple* Agents

You're probably thinking to yourself that you should pick the first agent that comes along. After all, we're all the same, right? ..... The answer is that you couldn't be more *WRONG!*

Imagine that you're out driving around on a Sunday afternoon looking at homes. You find a home that you really, really like. It's in the right neighborhood, and the yard has excellent curb appeal. Naturally, you want to find out more!

You decide to call the agent whose sign is in the yard. You meet with that agent, because you think they are the only one who can show you the house. *WRONG.*

Nowadays, most agents are part of the MLS (multiple listing system). That means that any of us can show almost any property out there.

So, BEFORE you call a total stranger whose phone number was on the sign, do a little research!

(One reason agents love "getting listings" is that yard signs generate lots of phone calls! The more yard signs they have, the more leads they get.)

Having Only One Option Is Not And Option

Friends, I beg you: before making what will probably be the largest financial decision of your life, INTERVIEW SOME AGENTS!

Now, I'm not saying you should automatically hire *me*, Randi Lynn Kroll. Don't get me wrong—I would love to have the opportunity of working with you. Maybe we would be a great fit! I sure hope so. But you should *always* do some research before hiring a real estate agent. It's a big decision!

I don't know of any businesses that hire the first person that applies for a job. Nope, that's not how it works. Usually the competition for job openings is fierce. The company's HR director will sort through dozens of resumes, and choose only a handful to actually come in for an interview. <u>Only then will they select the very best candidate.</u>

Don't you think you should put a little thought into who *you* hire?

ALWAYS, ALWAYS, ALWAYS ask for testimonials.

Testimonials are the best kind of research you can do. Take everything the agent says with a grain of salt. *Of course* they'll say good things about themselves. And that goes for me, too! Don't take my word for it; check out what my clients are saying about me!

I have a special website with personal testimonies of clients in the Will and Cook County areas talking about their experiences working with me. These are *testimonies that the clients submitted after we closed on their home*—I didn't tell them what to say, and I had no idea what they wrote until I saw the testimony arrive in my email. These reviews represent people's honest opinions about me.

Like I said, testimonials are the best kind of research you can do!

You can check out my testimonies online by
visiting: **www.SellYourHomeQuigley.com**

Make sure the agent you pick knows the market. And I mean really, truly, *knows the market*. A rookie agent might be able to memorize "knowledge" by doing a few minutes of research on MLS statistics, but is this really *wisdom*?

Don't be someone else's learning curve!

- Are they local?
- How long have they lived in your area?
- Are they full time?
- Do they have advanced credentials?
- Do they come across as trustworthy?
- Are they able to answer your questions without hesitation?

4. Rushing Your Buying Decision "Because There's Other Offers"

Let me tell you about a "trick" some agents pull.....

Let's say you are out house hunting and you find one you really like. Naturally, you want to be able to check on some details before you write an offer. No one wants to rush into a buying decision on something as expensive as a home! I mean, seriously—most people spend a few days doing online research of what *television* they're going to buy! With that in mind, you should NEVER make an impulse purchase when it comes to real estate. The stakes are simply too high. You're probably sitting there reading this thinking,

"Well, duh! I knew that." All I can say is that you'd be surprised how many people get caught up in a whirlwind of emotions and make irrational decisions.

Think of how emotionally invested you can get when watching real estate TV shows like *House Hunters*.

You think to yourself, "NO! Don't buy *that* house. Are they honestly not thinking at all? Buy *this* one!" It's easy to get excited about buying a home, even when it's not yours.

That being said, if you've never experienced the thrill of shopping for a home, the emotions are exponentially higher when it's not some stranger on TV.

It's *your* home that will be paid for with *your* money. All of a sudden, emotions come into play! And, as is usually the case, savvy real estate agents understand the subconscious psychological forces that make otherwise smart people do dumb things.

Here's an example:

The agent gets pushy and tells you to hurry **because there's another offer coming in, and you don't want to miss out on this one!**

I'll be blunt. Whenever I hear that "there's another offer coming in," I'm immediately skeptical.

When you hear the sellers tell you to *hurry and make an offer,* all sorts of things are running through your mind…

"What's the condition of the roof?"

"I wonder if there's hidden mold damage anywhere."

"I really genuinely do like this house, but I feel rushed."

Many buyers will hear this and their emotions get the best of them—they make a rushed decision and place an offer. This ploy works because the human brain is wired to fear loss more than it desires gain. Psychologically, it's more traumatic to lose something we already have than to not gain something we never had in the first place. You might be thinking "Well Randi, that doesn't make any sense. You never owned the home, so you weren't really losing it!"

Sort of.

When a showing goes well and buyers really like a home, they start to picture themselves in it. They visualize it being their home. They really truly do think it is their home! So when they hear the seller's agent say, "Hurry and make an offer, there is another buyer interested," alarm bells start to go off in their heads.

It would be emotionally traumatic to lose out on their dream home (never mind the fact that there's probably ten other homes out there that could be their "dream home").

The problem is that every once in a while, there actually *is* another offer on the table. Unfortunately, it's a perfect example of the boy who cried wolf. How can you really know?

My advice in situations like this is to ask yourself, *If this home was priced $20,000 higher than it currently is, would I still want it?* And at this point, if you still are unsure, what I suggest is before making an offer to doing a second showing that day. Or if there are other appointments scheduled after, I suggest to even sometimes cancel those and just spend more time at that home you fell in love with. It is very important that you feel confident when making the offer on your home. Once the offer is accepted you are legally entered into a binding contract, once signed.

This question is a good test on whether or not the home is truly perfect for you. If it is really your *dream home*, you will be willing to spend the extra money to make sure it's yours. If not, keep looking. There will be other homes you "fall in love with." Trust me.

Most people are not willing to slightly "overpay" for a home unless they are 100% convinced, beyond a shadow of a doubt, that this is their DREAM HOME. In that case, buyers will do pretty much anything to win the bidding war.

So the next time you hear, "Hurry and write an offer, there are other offers on the table," remember to ask yourself: would I be willing to pay an extra $20,000 for this home?

If not, keep looking!

No
Place
Like
Home

Trust me on this one......... people make decisions emotionally, and then attempt to justify those decisions with logic. This is one reason it's so important to have a trustworthy agent that sees when you are getting prematurely "excited" about a property, and can bring you back down to Earth.

It may be okay to make an emotionally impulsive decision on what to have for dinner, but it's probably not a good idea on a $150,000 (or more) purchase!

Anyways, back to the story...

Two weeks later, you find out that there really was no other interest and it's a ploy that agent uses to get his listings sold. Ugh. You move on and find another property. You LOVE this one!

Not learning from your first mistake, you call the agent on the sign.

After touring the home, your emotions are escalating. This home has all of your must-haves! It's got an open concept floorplan, spacious backyard, and the kitchen is newly updated. You decide this is *the one.*

Again, this agent says you will need to make an offer within the next 24 hours because "there is already one serious offer on the table."

Thinking that you won't be outsmarted this time, you call their bluff. *Except they're not bluffing.* There actually was a serious offer, and you lose out on this one!

You scramble, trying to offer more than asking price, throwing in every possible incentive to get that seller to take your offer. TOO

LATE! Contracts are legal and binding. The seller had to keep the original offer.

Lesson learned.

5. Losing Money By Ignoring The Power Of Negotiation

"In business as in life, you don't get what you deserve, you get what you negotiate." –*Chester Karrass*

Earlier, we touched on *location, location, location.*

Well, there's another word you need to commit to memory: *negotiate, negotiate, and negotiate!*

To avoid leaving money on the table, you'll need an experienced agent who understands the "art" of negotiation. For the most part, the skill of negotiating is something that is developed through experience. Like most things in life, the more you do it, the better you will get.

And that brings up an important question: **how are you supposed to develop the skill of negotiation when you will probably only buy/sell a few homes in your lifetime?**

The answer is simple: you need to trust the experience of your real estate agent.

I have participated in numerous amounts of negotiations. I have represented both sides of the table: buyers *and* sellers. When you consider how many deals I've been involved with, doesn't it make sense to rely on the experience of your agent?

In fact, this is how free enterprise works! In a free country, everyone gets really good at one specific thing. Economists call this process "specialization" or the "division of labor."

The entire point of a free economy is that people specialize in something, and then rely on other people to do what they're *not* experts at. This is why I'm more than happy to pay plumbers, auto mechanics, and carpenters to do their respective jobs—I sure as heck wouldn't be able to figure it out! And it's why they rely on *me* when it comes to buying and selling real estate.

It *pays* to use experts. And here's why an expert negotiator can save you so much money (or make you money, depending on how you look at it) there is no other activity, on a per hour basis that can generate the returns of good negotiating.

If you think doctors or lawyers make good money, consider this: they usually make a few hundred bucks an hour. Let's say $200. At the rate of $200/hour, it would take 25 hours to generate $5,000 (before taxes and all of that stuff). So a lawyer has to work 25 hours to earn $5,000, assuming they are billing $200/hour.

For the average middle class family in Will County buying a $200,000 home, you could "earn" $5,000 in two hours of negotiations. **That's $2,500 per hour.**

Whoa.

If you're buying a home, and you negotiate that the seller pays all closing costs (commission, home inspection, bank fees, etc), that can *easily* add up to $5,000.

Maybe you can get them to lower their price by $2,500 and agree to cover $2,500 of your closing costs... .....you just earned

$5,000! EVERYTHING is negotiable. The appliances, artwork, furniture, closing costs, home inspection, moving expenses, you name it. It all depends on your creativity.

Keep an open mind, and find a win-win solution!

You should know that the more expensive the home, the easier it is to "make money" during negotiations. On higher priced luxury homes, it's not uncommon for people to negotiate in $25,000 increments.

"I'll give you $650k."

"Nope, I need $715,000."

"Well, how about $675k?"

"Could you do $690,000?"

When you really stop and think about it, this is *crazy!* The average American earns around $30,000 per year, and in many real estate deals that much money can be made or lost in a split second decision. And it all depends on how skilled you are at negotiating.

For the average person, there is no easier way to earn money than developing solid negotiation skills. Period.

And if you aren't the type of person that feels "comfortable" negotiating, this is yet another reason why it's so important to work with a real estate agent you *trust.*

In many situations, a real estate agent can save you more money during negotiations than you actually pay them in the commission fee. So it actually costs you money to not work with a professional agent!

Let Us Never
Negotiate Out Of Fear.

But Let Us Never
Fear To Negotiate

- JFK

When I am negotiating out contract, whether it be with my sellers or my buyers, it is very important to be well educated. For example, when coming in with an offer from a buyer's perspective, what a good agent needs to do is study the market. She needs to provide comparable properties in the market that justify the price that you are offering. When you come in strong, with a story and documentation supporting your offer, now you have the upper hand. Take control of the situation. Many times we see offers come in on our own personal listings, to what we call "low ball" offers with nothing supporting why they asked the value they did. We often, as well, see offers with no preapproval, so how do we even know that the potential seller is able to financially purchase this home? This is why having a Realtor who is detailed orientated, dedicated, and who knows the market is a very crucial.

If you buy/sell a few homes over the course of your lifetime, it's not unrealistic to say that you could earn (or loose) $100,000 based on how skilled of a negotiator you are. Think about how that will affect your retirement lifestyle, your kids' college savings, or the amount you can donate to your church!

Moral of the story? Learn how to make money at the negotiating table!

PS

If your agent is knowledgeable, he or she will also tell you when you SHOULD write that full price offer. There *are* times that it's actually necessary. If a property truly is a high demand property (maybe in foreclosure, an estate sale, or other special circumstances), it could be priced to sell quickly.

A perfect Example; I recently sold a Townhome in Leighlinbridge in Manhattan to one of my clients. Please note that I also represent a Builder in Manhattans New Construction (currently as I write this book), so I am very familiar with the market in that area. When browsing through the new active listings that morning, as I normally do, I came across this townhome VERY competitively priced. About $50,000 less than what my New Construction was being sold at. My client immediately contacted me and I got him into this townhome hours later. He fell in love and we knew that he at that point should put in a full price offer. He did and he wound up getting his dream townhome. With this all being said, there are certain times when negotiating can actually hurt you. This is why having a realtor who is experienced and familiar with the market can really be beneficial. If my client had put in an offer lower and another offer came in higher during this negotiating period, he could have lost this perfect townhome for him.

Occasionally, those properties *do* get multiple offers on them. You may be coached to offer more than the asking price. This can happen! Again, I can't stress enough the importance of having the right person giving you advice.

As I've stated like fifty times in this book, it's all about TRUST. You have to *trust* and feel comfortable with your agent! If you don't…..find a new agent!

6. Being Intimidated By "The Numbers" (And How To Make Over $100,000 In 20 Years Or Less By Buying Instead of Renting)

"An investment in knowledge pays the best interest" - Benjamin Franklin

Don't be blinded by numbers.

What do I mean by that? Instead of seeing the big price tag, think about *affordable monthly payments.*

Remember: if you buy a house for $180,000, you aren't expected to write one big check for $180k. Nope—you make monthly payments! So instead of focussing about the final sales price, think about the "price" of your monthly payments. Can you afford them? If so, don't let the *big number* intimidate you.

And, really, this is truly a miracle from a historical perspective. For centuries, the average person lived in total poverty. Without our modern financial system that allows people to make affordable monthly payments, hardly anyone would be a homeowner. That's why many people define homeownership as **the American dream.**

I mean, think about it: even for a "starter" home priced at $80,000, how long would it take you to save up the entire $80,000?

You could probably do it, but it would take years... ... probably *decades.* Is it worth it to you to wait *decades* to invest in a home? Probably not.

If you're 30 years old right now, you might be sixty before you finally have saved up enough money to buy a house. That's a pretty big price to pay!

Without getting too philosophical here, the one thing you can't get more of is *time*. Everything else in life can be replaced: cars, clothes, jobs, computers, etc. But even the richest man on Earth cannot buy himself another year if he is dying. Time is not unlimited. It's a finite resource. It's the one thing you can't buy more of.

Time Has A
Wonderful Way
Of Showing Us
What Really Matters

You can't exchange dollars for more time… … …*or can you?*

When you agree to finance a home purchase by paying for it with a "mortgage," you are essentially trading dollars for time.

You are agreeing to pay a little bit more (what we call "interest") for the privilege of owning a home NOW, instead of having to wait until you've saved up enough money to write a check for the entire amount. And that could be *decades* away.…

For many people, they will never have enough money saved up to buy a house. For example, if you're making $25,000/year, you will probably never be able to save up $100,000 to buy a house. After all of your living expenses are factored in (taxes, insurance, gas, food, etc), there's simply not a lot of money left over every month. It would be extremely difficult, if not downright impossible, to save up $100,000 to buy a house without a mortgage.

That's why mortgages are so amazing! It allows the average American to invest in homeownership by making monthly payments. Most people would agree that they'd rather pay some interest on their monthly payments to actually *own* a home, rather than renting for years and years and years.

Oh, and did I mention that when you rent, there is an "opportunity cost" to that money?

Let's say it takes you twenty years to save up $100,000 to buy a house. This means that you're saving about five thousand dollars a year, or $416 per month. **After 20 years of saving $416 per month**, you finally have enough money in your savings account to go out and buy a $100,000 house!

But look at the *opportunity cost* of the situation... ... instead of saving that $416 every month in a savings account (which pays little to no interest) how else could you have invested that money?

Imagine that when you started saving your $416/month you were 25 years old. This means that you'd be 45 by the time you're able to buy your house! And you won't be living in a high-end luxury home... ... $100,000 will buy you a small American starter home or condo in let's just say Tinley Park.

With a budget of $100,000, you won't have high-end appliances, newer flooring, an updated kitchen, modern bathrooms, a big yard, or any of that stuff. So keep that in mind....

Here's the **opportunity cost** of the situation: during the twenty years you were saving up $416/month, you needed to live somewhere. You probably rented. Let's say you were spending $500 on rent (most people spend more than that!).

You've probably thought about this before, but it's worth repeating: renting is like flushing money down the toilet!

When you pay rent to the landlord (fancy term for whoever owns the home), you are essentially paying his bills, his mortgage, his expenses, etc.

But you never see that money again. It's not like when you move out you can ask for all the rent money you've paid. If you pay $500/month in rent, as soon as you mail that check, it's *gone*. Forever.

This might scare you: for the 20 years you've been saving up money to buy a house, **you will spend about $120,000 on monthly rent!!!!!!!!**

Don't believe me? 20 years is 240 months. 240 months times $500/month equals $120,000. (and that is super low- on average a one bedroom apartment in New Lenox will cost you $700-900 a month, almost double!!)

Yikes.

Moral of the story? Clearly, it makes sense to focus on the *monthly payment.* NOT the actual sales price.

Yes, you will pay more than the "sticker" price once interest is factored in. And yes, some financial gurus like Dave Ramsey think it's a terrible idea to pay interest on a home (for the record, I *love* Dave Ramsey and most of his advice is spot on).

But once you factor in the opportunity cost of paying all of that rent money, the decision is easy: go buy a house!

Whenever you hear someone say that homeownership is "too expensive," train yourself to ask the question, *expensive relative to what.....renting?*

ESPECIALLY in the Will and Cook County areas, this is a no brainer!

In Will and Cook County, homes can be affordable enough that renting makes ZERO sense if, of course, you can buy. I know it's a pretty bold statement, but think about it: if you have the financial discipline and responsibility necessary to own a home, why would you pay rent money?

<u>When you pay rent, it's basically a 100% interest payment.</u> You are not paying any principal. You are not building any equity. Once that money is spent, it is gone.

This is not the case in all areas of the country. In some cities it actually makes financial sense to rent, because homes are so expensive (places like San Francisco, New York City, etc). In that case, there would actually be an opportunity cost of *not* renting. This is NOT true in Will and Cook County. Homes are very, very affordable here!

If you're paying $1000/month in rent, why not invest *that same amount of money* every month in a mortgage payment? In a very literal sense, it wouldn't cost you a single penny to become a homeowner (there *are* programs out there to buy a home with ZERO DOWN).

Sure, there will be costs associated with homeownership that don't exist for renters. Renters don't have to pay to reshingle a roof every 25 years, upgrade aging furnaces, or redo the siding. But renters *are* paying for these things, indirectly. The rent money they pay every month gives the homeowner the cash to make these improvements.

Wouldn't you rather be the one *receiving* money than sending it?

When you pay your own monthly mortgage, you're basically *paying yourself.*

After interest is deducted, the money you pay every month pays down the balance of your mortgage. It's really no different from depositing that money in a savings account every month!

Think about it: if you're renting for $1000 it equates to $12,000 per year. Wouldn't you rather have that $12,000 in *your* "savings account" than the landlord's?

By buying instead of renting, you are spending the same amount of money—but instead of that cash going to the landlord it's being deposited into your home equity "savings account."

Eventually, you'll pay the mortgage off entirely and there won't be any more payments!

The $120,000 you would have paid is now cash in your pocket—the money you would have spent on renting all those years.

I mean, seriously! What would you do with an extra $120,000?!!

Unless you plan on moving out of the area in the foreseeable future, there is really no reason to rent.

I would say that the average New Lenox couple can expect to pay about $1400/month in rent. **That same $1400 of monthly rent would buy a $200,000 house if you were making a mortgage payment instead of paying rent.**

(assuming 5% interest rates and a standard 30 year mortgage)

Yes, there will be other expenses. Property taxes, home maintenance, etc. But keep in mind that when you are renting, you are indirectly paying for all of these things anyways. Where

Home Ownership
Has Always Been
Classified As
The American Dream

do you think the landlord gets the money to pay for all of these expenses—*you*!

Now, you probably think I'm biased because I'm a real estate agent. That's probably true…..I'm passionate about real estate! But you cannot ignore the simple math.

Would you rather pay $1400 every month in rent, or make $1400 mortgage payments on a $200,000 house? One path guarantees you will live your entire life month to month, just trying to scrape by with enough money to pay the bills. One path leads you to financial freedom. Which one will *you* choose?

It's a no brainer!

So if you're looking for a house and you put a certain dollar amount in your head as the "maximum" amount you are willing to spend, you could be missing out on some great opportunities! Many buyers, even before checking with their loan officer, decide what they want to spend. They let the "big number" get in the way.

Why? **Because it intimidates them.** They get scared. They can't conceptualize paying that much money for something—it just *feels* like a big number.

For instance, they will think about a $150,000 house and only see that big dollar amount. To make matters worse, they will figure out how much interest they will pay on that amount, over the next 30 years.

It seems like a logical thing to think about… …and 30 years seems like a ridiculously long ways away!

Instead of stressing about the big number, focus on the affordable monthly payments. Are you comfortable with *that* number? If so, buy the house!

With todays interest rates being incredibly low (which could change by the time you're reading this book), you would be surprised at how low the payments really are.

Let's say you've decided that you don't want to spend a dime more than $150,000. But a house comes along that's listed at $169,500. It is absolutely *perfect*. It's your dream home. Your real estate agent tells you that you can probably get it for $160,000. *But that's $10,000 over your limit.* You don't have an extra $10,000 laying around!

Instead of looking at the sales price, focus on the monthly payment. Especially when interest rates are reasonable, the difference in monthly payment between a $150,000 and $160,000 mortgage is... ... .about $50 a month.

Can you handle an extra $50/month to live in your dream home? For most of us, the answer is YES!

Don't let a fear of big numbers intimidate you! Focus on a monthly payment that you can comfortably afford.

7. Having Unrealistic Expectations With A Smaller Budget

Let me tell you about some first time homebuyers I worked with....

"David" and "Emily" (not their real names) wanted to look at homes in a certain area and were on a tight budget. Keep in mind it was their very first home, so they weren't spending $250,000. Well, they weren't spending even *close* to that.

To be honest, they weren't even spending *half* of that.

But they were used to spacious, luxurious homes (both came from somewhat wealthy families), so they had **completely unrealistic expectations.** They were assuming they could buy $200,000 worth of house for a little over $100,000. I knew from the start this would be an interesting house hunting process!

David and Emily needed to become a little more aware of the Real Estate Market. The first time we went out for coffee at the Banana café in Orland Park (and OMG their Smoothies are Ah-Maze-Ing!!), I tried to explain this to them. They didn't really listen to me when I tried to tell them that their wish list of "must haves" would make it challenging to find a home that has everything they need but I reinsured them that I would do my best to try to help find them a home that would meet *most* of their needs.

They wanted four bedrooms, newer hardwood floors, an updated kitchen, a modern master bath suite, and yard "suitable for entertaining."

I asked them to take out a piece of paper right then and there and write down their *wish list* in a priority order, marking what they would like the most on top and going down the list from there....

That first meeting at the Banana Café didn't go very smoothly. They claimed to "understand" my concerns, but tried to convince me that if I looked hard enough, I would find the perfect home for them. *I was so determined to try my best to find them their perfect home...*

Anyways, we started to take a look at the current homes on the market within their budget. We must have looked at over 20 homes. They were absolutely *determined* to live in the same area as some of their friends, but honestly, we couldn't find anything in their price range that even came close to *remotely* satisfying their wish list.

The homes that *were* in their price range needed extensive repairs—repairs that would require money David and Emily did not have at the moment, unfortunately.

I recommended to them to possibly *modify* their home search. After months of looking for houses, they decided to expand their home search and ended up purchasing a beautiful home, at a price well under their budget, in a neighboring town... ...*that was nicer than what any of their friends had.*

As I have stated before, keep an open mind.

This is more important than ever when you're buying your first home, and you're used to living in somewhat nicer housing. I get this a lot with buyers that are in their 20's. Even the college dorms today are pretty nice, so many of these first time homebuyers have a completely unrealistic expectation of what a "starter home" is all about.

If you're 20-something years old and reading this, pay attention!

The entire concept of a starter home is pretty self-explanatory: it's a home for you to "start" your home ownership experience. It won't be luxurious. It probably won't be spacious. It

The Secret Of Getting Ahead Is Getting Started

won't have a newly updated kitchen or a beautiful bathroom like you see in the home and decorating magazines. A starter home is usually small (two or three bedrooms), and has one bathroom. Sometimes two.

In the Will and Cook Counties (and surrounding communities) I would classify anything around $120,000 or less as a starter home.

A starter home will allow you to build a solid credit history, because the monthly payments *should* be extremely affordable. **Especially in Will County!** Houses here are incredibly affordable relative to renting.

As I've stated elsewhere in this book, this is NOT TRUE IN OTHER AREAS OF THE COUNTRY. In fact, usually when I go out of the area (or out of state) to visit my sister in New York or other family out of state and whatnot, my friends and family are absolutely *shocked* when I tell them how affordable homes are in my market.

The usual reply I get is, "Why would ANYONE rent? If homes are that cheap, everyone should buy!"

All I can do is nod my head in agreement.

And truth be told, it's a great feeling knowing that you have money left over every month. Many people make the mistake of buying exactly what they can "afford," so there's basically zero dollars leftover every month for entertainment, vacations, etc. Trust me—this will really stress you out!

It's better to buy an affordable starter home that's well *beneath* your budget, and have plenty of "breathing room" every month.

You'll be a happier person, I guarantee it. As your career develops and you start earning more money, *then* you can look into buying a nicer home with a larger mortgage payment.

Do NOT buy a "reach" home (where you're reaching a bit beyond what you can actually afford) as your first home. This is a HUGE mistake.

Remember: a starter home is all about building a solid financial foundation.

A starter home will not *only* help you build a solid credit history. It's a great learning experience! Owning a home gives you an entirely new perspective on "living." When you own the house you live in, you will notice things you didn't notice before.

- The condition of the siding.
- The condition of the shingles on the roof.
- The efficiency of your "HVAC" systems.

I could probably rattle off a dozen more, but here's what I'm getting at: home owners have to be responsible for many things that tenants take for granted. This awareness gives you a new perspective on the true cost of having a brand new kitchen, updated bathroom, new flooring, etc.

Homeownership is a crash course in the value of a hard earned dollar.

Tenants will often complain that the kitchen is ugly, the bathroom needs to be updated, or the carpets need replacing. When you become a homeowner, you realize how expensive this stuff is, and all of a sudden it makes sense to you why most landlords don't spend gobs of money updating their properties—it simply doesn't make financial sense!

Doing a minor kitchen renovation could set you back $10,000. Updating a bathroom can easily cost a few grand! New flooring adds up quickly, too. For a landlord to justify investing this much money back into a house, he or she would need to charge a lot more in rent... ... ... which *very few* renters are willing to pay.

Once you own your own home, all of these things start to make sense.

Instead of having vague thoughts in your head like "I deserve a new kitchen," you start to count the cost. It teaches you the value of a dollar! And it psychologically prepares you to buy a "nicer" home in the future *by understanding what you're paying for.*

Owning a home will make you a more responsible person, period. It teaches you to look at things from a value perspective instead of an entitlement perspective. And that's a good thing!

With any luck, your home will appreciate while you own it. So not only will you build up equity by paying down the mortgage every month, you will increase your net worth through appreciation of your home's value (there are ways to "force" appreciation that I cover elsewhere in the book).

In summary, investing in a "starter" home is a very, very valuable thing to do. It will allow you to build your credit, become a more responsible person, and financially position you to invest in your "dream home" someday.

A journey of a thousand miles begins with a single step....

So don't let unrealistic expectations stop you from buying your first starter home!

8. Not Conducting A PROFESSIONAL Home Inspection

I'm not kidding, I could probably write an entire book on the subject of home inspections. So it'll be hard for me to stay focused and narrow this down to a few pages! *That's how important it is to have a home inspection.*

Seriously.

Years ago, from what I have heard numerous times now, home inspections weren't really that common. Sometimes a buyer would have a trusted friend take a look at the house (usually an electrician, plumber, or someone they knew with construction experience). It wasn't anything formal, and it didn't really affect the buying process one way or another. Homes were bought and sold like my first grade son trades his baseball cards.

Professional investors were much more likely to do their "due diligence" on a property, because they needed to know the deferred maintenance, future renovation expenses, etc.

But for the average residential homebuyer, **you basically had to trust that the seller wasn't hiding any problems.** And for many homes, that was quite a leap of faith.

Today, it's pretty much standard to have a professional home inspection before closing on a house.

If you don't already know, a home inspection involves a home inspector going through everything in the house and making sure there are no problems. The only thing a home inspector cannot do is check out what's inside the walls. Home inspectors will check the roof to see the condition of the shingles, they will check the siding, they will examine the walls and ceilings for signs of water leaks, they will check all sinks/faucets, they will check the power outlets, they will check the age/condition of the HVAC system components, etc. It's a very thorough investigation!

On an average size house, a home inspection will take approximately 2-4 hours.

Typically it costs $300 or $400 to have a professional home inspection. As I've said elsewhere in the book, this is ALWAYS negotiable.

Most of the time the buyer is the one who pays for the inspection.

Trust me on this one—it will be the best $400 you ever spend. I've had instances where a problem was discovered during the routine home inspection that potentially saved the buyer over ten thousand dollars!

<u>Personally, I wouldn't even CONSIDER buying a home without an inspection.</u>

You can breathe a sigh of relief once the home inspection report has been filed! The only thing a home inspector *can't* do is rip open the walls to see what's inside, or start tearing open the flooring. Other than that, the home inspection should reveal any potential problems, fixes, and repairs that need to be made before closing.

Following a home inspection, it's pretty common for a buyer to request that the seller make a few repairs prior to closing (problems that were discovered in the home inspection).

But let me be very, very, very clear on this: the home inspection is not meant to create a "laundry list" of repairs for the seller. Unless you're moving into a brand new home, there *will be* maintenance issues, things that need repair, etc. It's just a fact of life.

A good home inspector will coach you through all of this, and teach you how to be proactive when it comes to "preventative maintenance." Your car regularly needs oil changes, tire rotations, etc—so does your house! If you fell in love with a great used car, you wouldn't *not* buy it because it's in need of an oil change. The same goes for purchasing a house….don't let minor, correctable problems get between you and your dream home!

If the extent of the repairs is over a few hundred dollars, you may need to renegotiate the price if the seller isn't willing to make those repairs. Sometimes the seller will even give a credit at closing. Again, consult with your real estate agent and home inspector. It's ultimately up to you, but they will be able to provide you with the wisdom necessary to make the right decision.

And remember: everything is negotiable.

But, keep in mind, if you truly want the house, you won't allow a few minor repairs to stop you from buying the house.

In fact, I would venture to say that it's nearly impossible for a home inspection to *not* reveal things that need to be repaired.

It is almost guaranteed that the home inspector will discover problems with the home. When you hire a home inspector, you should EXPECT there to be problems detailed in the report. Usually, these problems are not a big deal.

Pay close attention here: because of potential liability, a home inspector is incentivized to make things sound worse than they probably are.

Consequently, many homebuyers get overwhelmed when they receive the home inspection: "Oh my Gosh! There are 4 missing shingles, the kitchen sink leaks, and one of the window needs to be replaced!"

At this point, you need to *slowwwwwwww down.*

Try to evaluate the situation logically and not emotionally. Replacing a few shingles, fixing a basic leak, and replacing a window is *not a big deal.*

Do NOT let the home inspection intimidate you or scare you. Know that the home inspection report will make it sound much worse than it actually is. It is their job to make sure they point out everything and anything that is not perfect in the home, for you.

You Have To Think
Anyways
So Why Not Think Big
And See The Big Picture

Now, don't misunderstand me—I'm not saying you should ignore the home inspection report. I *am* saying that you should look at the big picture.

Don't let a few imperfections scare you away. You will end up spending money on "maintenance" anyways... ...it's better to proactively find out then *react* to a problem that has compounded over time!

Can you think about the "band-aids" you have used to cover up little leaks, stains, or broken items? I have a pretty good story about that...

There was a house that I actually showed to my sister and brother in law, when they were in search of their very first home!! (I love working with First Time Buyers!!) Anyways, this home was a flip home. The home appeared to be Spotless and completely updated!

The ceilings were freshly painted. New Floors, New Appliances, New Everything pretty much, actually. The first time we viewed this home it was in the evening. From the looks of it, this may have been "the one!" My sister and Brother-In-Law were in no hurry and they decided to take some time to think about it some more. About two weeks later we scheduled a second showing to see this home in the day time. With that being said, what we saw at that showing was verrrrryyyyy different than what we saw the first time....

Downstairs while taking a look at the basement, I had noticed what appeared to be "Spots" on the white trim. Interesting, figuring it was a completely new renovated home. Why would they not have all the white trim painted ALL WHITE? Right? I looked a little further into it and noticed that ALL OVER THE ENTIRE

BASEMENT there was Mold peeking through the newly freshly painted home.

If the house was to sell within days of listing, as they probably had imagined, no one would have even seen this. Unless, of course, a good inspector had been hired!!

Now, here's my question: ***do you suppose that mold was New?***

Of course not! The seller painted over the mold area to try to cover it up instead of just remove it. Yet, since the home had been sitting vacant for months without selling, the mold started to come through in spots ALL OVER.

Needless to say, they walked from the property and decided not to write up and still, to this day, the home is not yet sold. (Again, as I write this book)

Had that happened after closing, the sellers would have ended up in court. As a seller, you are legally (and I would say *morally*) obligated to disclose any problems with the property.

By doing so, the buyers will need to sign off on it—and won't be able to come back and sue you for anything you disclosed. If it is ever proved that you knew about something and did NOT disclose it, you are in deep legal trouble.

Of course, the best thing to do is make the repairs.

Here's what you need to remember: I always, always, always recommend having a home inspection before buying a house. Just don't let the home inspection report scare you away from investing in the home of your dreams!

If you are looking for some referrals of Great Inspectors that I have worked with, please let me know. I can give you a few contacts of mine that I highly recommend.

9. Letting Friends, Family, And Other Non-Experts (That Generally Don't Know What They're Talking About) Influence *YOUR* Decision

"Don't let someone who gave up on their dreams talk you out of going after yours"

I'll try to keep this section short and sweet!

Do NOT allow unsolicited opinions from friends, family, or other non-experts to have too much influence on your home buying decision.

(The exception would obviously be if you have friends or family that work professionally in the real estate industry)

I've heard this too many times to count.....

Randi, our parents need to look with us!

If your parents will be living there with you, fine. No judgment.

If not, do some independent research on what YOU want, go house hunting, find your top 3 houses, THEN bring them in to look............after you've already toured the properties yourself.

I *completely understand* that you trust your parents' wisdom and experience. After all, they've probably bought/sold multiple homes, so they probably can provide some helpful long-term perspective. But that doesn't mean you abdicate all responsibility and decision making to them. Don't let them override you.

I see this all the time: a couple falls in love with a home. It's in their budget and it's in the right neighborhood. But the parents don't like it for some reason. Not wanting to insult their parents, the buyers walk away from a deal. After all, **they don't want to ask for their parents' advice and then ignore it.**

But keep in mind that *your parents are not real estate experts.*

If there is something inherently wrong with a deal, the real estate agent will advise you accordingly. If you like a home, the real estate agent thinks it's a good fit, and the bank agrees to finance the mortgage... ....do it! At that point, any other opinions are exactly that—*opinions.*

I mean, you wouldn't let your parents perform brain surgery on you just because they are your parents. The same goes for your friends, coworkers, or anyone else that feels the need to tell you what you should or shouldn't buy.

Politely thank them for their suggestions, and then do whatever you were going to do.

I am *not* trying to disrespect parents. I am one. However, I have had clients LOVE a home fully and completely. They, then, set up a second showing before actually putting up an offer on the property and at this time the parents join. A few times the clients actually leave the home, less excited about the property they had once LOVED. They choose to hold off writing up an offer. The property sells that next week and the clients regret the fact that they let their dream home go.

Point being, this is your home. Your mortgage. It should be something you love.

This is where it's most important to find an agent you TRUST. This is a constant theme throughout the book: finding an agent you *trust*.

As a parent, if you see the top 3 homes your child selected...... and you hate them all.....talk to the agent!

Part of the problem may be price range. Don't worry if your son or daughter can't afford their dream home at age 25!

It's far better for them to build a solid credit history, learn the ropes of homeownership, and become a financially responsible young adult than it is to buy a "stretch" home at the top of their budget that leaves them broke at the end of every month because of an expensive mortgage payment.

The other issue I sometimes see with well-intentioned parents is comparing the current market to what it was when *they* purchased.

I can't tell you how many times I have heard, "Well when we bought our house in 1970, it was only $40,000 and it was twice this size!"

Here are my thoughts... Ready... ... inflation. Most everything was "cheaper" in 1970 because the dollar was worth more. That doesn't mean your son or daughter is getting ripped off buying their home. If it's priced well *relative to the market right now*, that's all you need to worry about!

Advice is good, but *don't make unrealistic comparisons.* You may just end up getting frustrated instead of excited... and this is such an exciting time for you!

10. Expecting The Homebuying Process To Be As Fun As It's Portrayed To Be On *HGTV* (The REAL LIFE Process Of House Hunting Is Way More Confusing, Stressful, and Difficult Than It Looks On Television....... Why You Shouldn't Let This Intimidate You)

In the next few pages, I'm going to reveal a secret about how hit TV shows like "House Hunters" are set up behind the scenes.

... ...you didn't *actually* think it was real, did you?

But first, some honest advice about house hunting.

The home buying process doesn't always go smoothly. And especially if it's your first time buying a home, the process can be downright *scary.*

I'll be brutally honest here: it's intimidating.

There are lots of forms to sign. Lots of paperwork. Lots of meetings.

It will seem like the bank wants all sorts of things from you: recent paycheck stubs, last year's taxes, a credit report, etc.

You *may* get stressed out. Try to come to terms with this before you get started. *However, it is the job of your Realtor to explain the process to you and be there every step of the way.*

All sorts of things will be running through your mind....

Title insurance.....wait, what's a title? And what am I insuring?

And I heard something in the newspaper about a property tax levy. How do I register to pay property taxes? And I don't even know what a levy is. Doesn't it have something to do with rivers and dams? I don't think there's any rivers or dams in New Lenox where I live. But I guess I'm not sure. Which reminds me, should I get flood insurance? Is that even a problem in Will County? Hmmmmmmm... ....

Speaking of insurance, I need to insure my home! Where do I go for that? Does it cover fire damage? Hail? What if we have a water leak? And how much does it cost?

Cost.....yikes....I wonder what utilities will cost every month. Will someone send me a bill? Or do I have to go somewhere to pay it?

And how will I pay the mortgage every month? Do I have to drive to the bank every 4 weeks? Can I set that up on autopay?

I also remember something about a deed. I have no idea what that is. Does that cost extra? And closing costs.....how much will those be? And what exactly am I paying for? What is closing, anyway? Is something open that needs to be shut?

As you can see, if you've never bought a home before, the process can be confusing!

Here's my advice to you: accept the fact that at some point, you *May* be overwhelmed. *You May be stressed out.* You *May* be confused. You *May* be afraid to ask "questions." You *May* start to experience doubts. You *May* question whether or not buying a home was such a good idea.

This is completely normal. *Everyone* experiences this.

Trust me on this one: it's much easier to navigate the home buying process when you are mentally prepared.

If you acknowledge ahead of time that there will be things you don't understand, you won't let it dominate your thoughts.

Real life is not like HGTV. However, this makes it even more important that you have a GREAT relationship with your Realtor.

Here's an insider secret about how most of these real estate reality TV shows actually work: it's all staged!

With the popular show *House Hunters*, the couple has already purchased the home they end up "selecting" in the end. *Sorry if I just ruined the fun for you.*

On shows like *House Hunters*, they are basically pretending the entire time that they are looking at homes. In reality, they've already chosen the home they are going to live in. They've actually already bought it!

The show is usually filmed after the fact, and then they go out "house hunting" and pretend that they haven't actually decided. One of the homes they tour is, in fact, already theirs.

It would be like watching the *Bachelor* knowing that prior to filming, the bachelor was already married to the show's "winner." It's all a pre-planned show.

To put it bluntly, *it is fake*, unfortunately.

This is because in the real world, it's not all sunshine and rainbows all of the time...

Most couples on *House Hunters* look at 3 homes and, magically, find their dream home. Every single time. I mean, seriously, does anyone believe that this is legit?

House hunting is more complex than the 30 minutes of edited footage you see on TV.

There might be bumps in the road. Actually, let me rephrase that. There WILL BE BUMPS IN THE ROAD. In fact, there might be some 12 inch potholes deep enough to get lost in.

Figuratively, not literally.

Whether it's a home inspection issue, a financing issue, or just not finding what you're looking for, try to be as *patient* as you can. Always remember your goal.

That goal may be a variety of things... you want to be a home OWNER. The financial security that comes with owning your own home, and the *feeling* of owning your home... .....will make everything worth it.

Trust me!

Keep Calm

And

TRUST

Your

REALTOR

11. Not Signing A Contract
With A Buyer Agent

I'll get straight to the point: do NOT *always* simply call the phone number on the yard sign. *If you do not have an agent already, and call off the sign once, fine. However, it would be in your best advantage as a buyer to try to find one agent and work with them. They will have our*

Why? The phone number on the yard sign is the listing agent's phone number. The listing agent is contractually obligated to represent the best interests of the seller first, at the time you call them. Not you as a potential buyer just calling off their sign.

This means that they won't really give you objective information, advice, or insights on the property. They have one goal and one goal only: sell the house for the sellers.

When you are working directly with one agent they will put you first. What this means is that they are obligated to do what is best for *you*. They will research homes for *you*. They will submit offers for *you*. They will negotiate for *you*. They will do what's in your best interest, not the seller's. This is a huge advantage!

And the best part? The buyer's agent only gets paid when you actually buy a house (usually their commission is paid *by the seller*).

YOU are their customer. Not the seller. They want to do what's right for *you*. If they don't, they won't get paid!

Unfortunately, many buyers simply do a few hours of online research, drive around and look at some properties, then call the number on the sign. Many times they will talk with 5 different agents in a month!

Guess what? Most agents really aren't interested in working with you if you aren't "loyal" to them. This isn't because they feel entitled—it's just not a good use of their time to spend hours and hours with someone that might end up buying a home with another agent. It would be like a car salesman spending lots of time with a customer, taking them on multiple test drives, helping them understand the financing, and then... .....the customer buys the car through another salesman.

Clearly, real estate agents don't want to invest a bunch of time and money into a client that views the various agents as interchangeable commodities.

When you sign a buyer agreement contract to work exclusively with one agent, that agent is now incentivized to work for *you*. They will have *your* best interests in mind.

And remember: **they don't get paid until you actually buy a new home!**

In fact, I can't think of a good reason why you would *not* work with a buyer agent!

Of course, it's important to make sure you choose the agent that's right for you. I've said it 100x in this book, but it's vitally important that you *trust* your agent. That's what it ultimately boils down to. When you trust that your agent will do what is right for you, it takes a lot of stress out of the home buying process!

And to check out some testimonials of clients that bought and sold real estate with me, take a look at my site:

www.SellYourHomeQuigley.com

12. Not Getting Pre-Qualified For A Mortgage

I can't think of a single good reason why you would NOT want to be prequalified for a mortgage. It makes the house hunting process so much easier!

In one of my print ads promoting this book, I stated that after reading the book, you would know the "number one mistake made by homebuyers."

Well, this is it.

The number one mistake made by homebuyers is NOT getting prequalified for a mortgage.

When you get prequalified, everything else falls into place. You know exactly how much you can spend, so you don't waste time looking at homes you can't afford (online or in person). This will make *your* life less stressful, *and* your real estate agent's.

Getting pre-qualified is the most important step to house hunting!

There's nothing more disheartening than to fall in love with a house.....only to find out that you can't afford it. It's even more humiliating when you place an offer "contingent" on financing..... and the financing falls through.

To get prequalified, the first step is finding a loan officer that you can TRUST. And it might not be at "your" bank.

Just like finding the right real estate agent, finding the right loan officer is really important! They are not all the same. It's worth your time to "shop around" and figure out which loan officer best fits your personality, needs, etc.

Sometimes you will really like your bank, but you don't "click" with the loan officer there. Sometimes the opposite happens— you don't really like a particular bank, but you enjoy working with a loan officer that works there. My advice would be to go with whatever loan officer you are most comfortable with.

(It's more accurate to say that you are working with the specific, individual loan officer than you are working with the overall banking entity)

It should be someone you can actually look at face to face—be careful of online financing! There are many "big name" companies out there like *Quicken Loans* that are probably reputable and trustworthy, but I still feel that you will highly benefit from working with an actual person that you can physically pick up the phone to call or drive to and see.

They are not ALL bad, but why risk it?

I can virtually guarantee that you will be much happier (and less stressed) if you work with a local bank or lender that has a *physical presence* in your community. You're in luck, because there are many fantastic lenders in the Will and Cook County areas. You will have options when it comes to financing! Same goes for

Lenders as it does Real Estate Brokers, you need to find one that you feel comfortable with.

It's really nice to stop by your lender or bank while you're doing errands in town, and have a quick chat if you have a question. You can't do that when your mortgage is handled by an online finance company.

There's just something to be said about good old fashioned face-to-face conversation!

Unlike books, movie tickets, or other items commonly purchased online, a mortgage is difficult to process in the virtual world. It's simply too complex and personal of a process to be handled well online.

Maybe that will change in the coming years—I'm sure people were originally skeptical about many things that are sold online today. But right now (I'm writing this book in 2015), I advise my clients to avoid online mortgages.

It's simply too risky!

I have seen deals fall apart the day of closing. I have also seen "good deals" be everything BUT good. They have a way of sneaking in some last minute "surprise" closing costs. This is how they remain profitable even though their advertised mortgage rates *seem* like really good deals (usually better than the rates at local banks).

For example, instead of the $6500 you were "quoted," you get to the closing table and find out they have some extra fees tacked on.....and your closing costs are really closer to $8000!

It's usually a much better idea to "keep it local," and work with a local lender that is truly part of the community.

Local lenders have accountability and incentive to serve you and get the deal done in a timely manner—it's much easier to complain about bad service when it's a local company than it is with an unknown online company.

Local banks and lenders can't afford to have negative word of mouth circulate in a community, so they are usually dedicated to providing great service!

RUNNING

COMPS

is my

CARDIO

Dos and Don'ts for Choosing The Real Estate Agent That's Right For You

"You are a product of your environment, surround yourself with the BEST"

B uying a home is one of the most complex and expensive purchases you will ever make....and it's not a purchase I would recommend making on your own.

Unless you have direct experience in the real estate industry (maybe as a property investor, mortgage broker, lender, home inspector, etc), it will be extremely hard to "wing it."

And even if you have experience in real estate, you are still putting yourself at an *extreme* disadvantage by not being represented by a licensed agent (preferably a certified Realtor).

To avoid making expensive (potentially *very* expensive) mistakes, you have to understand our local market here in Will County, know where the inventory is, what the short term and long term trends are, how to negotiate, what contracts and inspections to perform, how to effectively market your listing or efficiently search for your new home.....the time you have to invest can cause you to pull out your hair if you don't know what you're doing!

Trust me on this one—something like 90% of "for sale by owners" eventually list their home with a licensed real estate agent. Why? Because eventually, they figure out it's a lot harder than it looks. Specifically, a lot more time consuming!

There is a reason we hire real estate agents. But whom should you choose? What should you look for in an agent? It's not an easy choice, but here are five things you *shouldn't* do and five things you *should* do.

1. *Don't* choose the first agent you meet

Let me ask you a question: would you marry the first person you met? Of course you wouldn't. The same logic applies when it comes to choosing a real estate agent ... even if the agent is a referral.

While it's not a life-long commitment like a marriage, buying or selling a home is a huge, high-stress endeavor (if you don't believe me, ask anyone who has bought or sold real estate). You want to make sure you've picked the *right* person to help you navigate those waters. And that person might not be me.

I'm not writing this book to convince you that **Randi Lynn is awesome** and all the other agents are terrible. Instead, I hope this book is a valuable resource that empowers you to ask the right questions and make a more informed decision. I wish I had a copy of this book back when I first started buying and selling homes.

Here's the bottom line: we have some amazing, highly professional agents here in the South and Southwest Suburbs of Illinois. I want to make sure you pick the agent that is right for *you*.

Get as many recommendations as you can, and take the time to interview several real estate agents. Ask each agent questions like these:

- Are you a member of the National Association of Realtors?
- Will you show me houses listed by other realty companies?
- How familiar are you with the area?
- What is your average list price/sales price ratio?
- What is the average DOM (days on market) of your listings?
- Can you provide a list of testimonials from satisfied clients? Make sure, too, that the testimonials come directly from a company that sends out feedback to the client. Feel free to check out mine at www.sellyourhomequigley.com
- What is your strategy/plan to help me find a home?
- Do you work weekdays and weekends?
- What makes you an expert on local real estate?
- Why should I choose you over other agents?

Compare the answers with your other interviews, and choose an agent who best matches your personality, style, goals, etc.

It's sad, but most people do more research on what car they want to drive than what real estate agent they work with. While car shopping, they'll do research online, physically go to a few dealerships, take a few test drives, compare and contrast, *then* they make a decision.

Very few people do this when it comes to buying/selling homes. They just call the number on a yard sign, or take a blind recommendation from a friend without doing any "due diligence."

Trust me—you'll be much happier with your buying/selling experience if you are happy with the agent you chose. Do some research!

2. *Don't* hire someone just because he or she says what you want to hear

You want an agent who will challenge you. Who will tell you when you are wrong. Who will keep you from making a huge (potentially six figure) mistake. Many agents are so concerned with not offending their clients that they are afraid to be honest with them. To me, this is really, really important.

If I were a buyer or seller, I would want an agent that was absolutely *brutally honest* with me.

I don't really care if a retail associate at Target or Best Buy sugarcoats a product, or tells me what I want to hear to massage my ego. If I end up making a dumb decision on a $50 item, it's not really a big deal. Even something more expensive like a TV is fine in relative to something like a car, or yet, a house. Life goes on....*but when it comes to the biggest investment of your life, you want to know exactly what you're getting into!*

Agents that are not brutally honest are doing you a HUGE disservice. They are afraid the client will get mad and fire them. Well, I would rather you fire me because I gave you honest advice (that may not be exactly what you want to hear at the moment)

than watch you make a mistake that costs you a lot of money.....
and then proceed to tell the whole town "how bad of an agent Randi
is." In a small town like New Lenox, word-of-mouth travels quickly.
Especially in the age of social media like Facebook!

I can't afford to let my clients make expensive, preventable
mistakes. And they *definitely* can't afford it!

Look for someone who is assertive but not obnoxious. Ask him
or her how they would respond if you wanted to make an offer on a
house they knew was way beyond your budget, make a lowball offer
in the wrong situation, or any other ethically difficult situation.

Long story short: a good agent does what is right for *your* wallet,
not theirs.

Respect Is Earned.

Honesty Is Appreciated.

Trust Is Gained.

Loyalty Is Returned.

3. Do Work with a Buyer Agent

Did you know that all real estate agents are deemed to be working for the seller *unless* there is a written agreement that says otherwise?

That's why a "Buyer Representation Agreement" is a smart move for anyone in the market to buy a home. There really aren't any exceptions to this....it is ALWAYS in your best interest to work with a buyer agent that is representing *you*—not the seller.

Buyer's agents come in a few flavors:

General Buyer Agent: Many real estate brokerages have designated buyer agents that primarily work with buyers. These agents usually don't have a lot of listings, so the potential for conflict of interest is a bit lower. Any agent or broker, however, can enter into a *Buyer Representation Agreement* with you to help you find a home and protect your interests.

Accredited Buyer's Representative: The ABR designation signals that an agent has taken advanced courses specific to buyer representation, and along with meeting other requirements has been accredited for working specifically with homebuyers.

Exclusive Buyer Agent: Exclusive buyers agents never work for sellers, because they don't take listings and neither does the brokerage they work for. Instead, these agents work *exclusively* for buyers.

This is the only form of buyer agency that completely eliminates a conflict of interest between your agent/broker and the seller.

If you're working with anyone other than an exclusive buyer agent, the possibility exists that you will want to buy a listing that is held by the agent you're working with or the brokerage firm that agent works for. This is a situation called **dual agency**, and it means that the seller has already received the bulk of the guidance from the brokerage, but your representation might become more "neutral."

Now, let me be very clear. I don't want you to misunderstand what I'm saying here: *there is absolutely nothing illegal or unethical about dual agency.* The agent just has to make sure that he or she has the written consent from both parties, however.

The only potential problem is that a real estate brokerage is put in a situation where it has to balance loyalties between both parties, which can lead to some sticky negotiating situations. Legally, the agent has to be careful to protect the rights of both parties involved.

Make sure there is an escape clause in your contract so that you don't get trapped into a shady long-term agreement with an agent you dislike. Personally, I always have flexibility with my clients and contracts. I don't want them to feel pressured into signing or agreeing to *anything.*

4. Don't hire agents who don't know how to negotiate

The real estate industry (everywhere, not just Will County) is full of part time, inexperienced real estate agents. These are the last people you want to help you buy your new home (and a good reason why you should choose a member of the *National Association of Realtors*).

But even for those who have made it a full-time career – and thoroughly enjoy what they do – if they are afraid of conflict and don't have sharp negotiation skills, they are not going to maximize your experience. And by that I mean "dollars"

Look for a real estate agent who's not afraid to make tough requests or knows how to deal with a lowball offer.

5. Do not chose an agent based solely on their production.

Every market has real estate *superstars*—agents that have figured out how to leverage their time and money so that they can generate hundreds of thousands of dollars (sometimes millions) in annual commissions.

I would suggest for you to think about what exactly that means for you, as the client. That might sound counter intuitive..... wouldn't a realtor have a better chance of being successful with you considering their wonderful track record?

Well, no, not really. You see, an agent may or may not have what you are looking for. You and that agent may define success very differently.

Sometimes, too, when working with some of these agents, you won't necessarily be dealing with that individual alone. Rather their assistants, etc.

What I pride myself on is always keeping all of my Real Estate Transactions personable. It is a very BIG DEAL to be Selling and Buying your home and I actually truly enjoy getting to know my clients and working side by side with them. The only time you may not hear from just me is when scheduling showings, because we do have a system that does that for us.

Please keep in mind that one agent may define success by the number of transactions he closes a month, the amount of commission he makes, the number of awards he's accumulated.

Another agent might define success with the number of healthy relationships she's built, satisfied clients she has, or the number of video testimonials she receives.

One agent is all about himself. The other is all about you. Choose the one who is in alignment with your personality and goals.

Again, I'm not saying "extremely high producing" real estate agents are to be avoided altogether. If they have high transaction numbers, *clearly they know what they are doing.* But you need to know what you're getting into! You don't want to be an anonymous "number" in their sales statistics.

And to achieve high "production" numbers (industry insiders use the word *production* to signify how much commission dollars they've "produced"), it's almost impossible to dedicate yourself to each and every client.

If an agent is all about **their** goals, it's hard for them to focus on **yours**.

Find an agent committed to *you.*

6. *Do* pick an agent who matches your personality needs

Good real estate agents approach the art of buying and selling houses differently because they know that each client is different in personality and needs. Some agents even specialize in dealing with particular client types.

In her New York Times article *Who's Got Your Back?*, Vivian S. Toy identifies four such real estate agents:

- **Hand-Holder** – This person will be slow to speak, slow to make a move, and will be patient when you have a thousand questions to answer. He won't mind answering the same questions ten times. He understands the anxiety behind buying a home and will help you calm down.
- **Authority** – This person is loaded with knowledge about the market and inventory, understands the ins-and-outs of real estate, and is confident in that knowledge and experience. She is a take-charge type.
- **Team** – This is a group of people who specialize in certain aspects of real estate, usually led by an authority (the face on all the promotional material). This team is on call at all hours – an efficient and effective, well-oiled machine. The only downside is you will never work with the person you met on your introductory visit (if you met him at all).
- **Legacy Broker** – This person is someone who has been the go-to person in a certain family or social circle. She values the relationship with the larger group, so you know she won't steer you wrong. However, this kind of agent is difficult to find ... and it's hard to get inside that inner circle.

These categories aren't definitive. Every agent is probably a mixture of each. But hopefully this gives you a *general* idea of how agents can have different personalities and approaches.

Personally, I would say I'm probably more of the *authority* type, with a little *hand holder* mixed in when I'm dealing with clients that have lots of questions (such as first time homebuyers).

7. *Do* choose a full-time, seasoned REALTOR

When it comes to buying or selling a home, you want an experienced, professional real estate agent by your side. As I've said elsewhere in the book, you want an agent that eats, breathes, and sleeps real estate. I would highly suggest working with an agent that is full time, though some part time agents are really good at what they do as well. However, Real Estate is not a 9-5 Monday through Friday job... heck its pretty much 24-7.

Full time agents have a few distinctive traits that set them apart from part-timers.

- They are career real estate specialists
- They will work to lower your risk
- They will work for you at their own risk
- They understand the current market
- They have and know inventory
- They understand the complexity of the transaction
- They have *wisdom* versus just *knowledge*.

Dedication
Is The Key
To Success.

Randi Lynn

In addition, look for agents with some additional training. Having various certifications doesn't guarantee an agent will be right for you (or even a good agent at all), but it at least shows that they are dedicated to professional development.

In addition to my Real Estate Career, I have my Bachelors in Business Administration with a Double Major in Marketing and Finance. I also have an Associate's Degree in Interior Design. I have a ton of formal education that I feel truly benefits what I am able to do for my clients, in the Real Estate World.

Here are a list of some other Real Estate Certifications. You know this when you see the acronyms behind their name. Here's what some of those acronyms mean:

- **CRS (Certified Residential Specialist)**: A network of 33,000 agents who receive tools and training to help buyers or sellers make the residential transaction as smooth as possible.
- **GRI (Graduate Realtor Institute)**: According to National Association of Realtors' website, GRI designees: *Have pursued a course of study that represents the minimum common body of knowledge for progressive real estate professionals, have developed a solid foundation of knowledge and skills to navigate the current real estate climate (no matter what the market condition), and act with professionalism and are committed to serving their clients and customers with the highest ethical standards.*
- **ABR (Accredited Buyer's Representative)**: Another designation that signals to buyers that a real estate agent is serious about honing their skills.
- **Certified *Realtor***: Many people mistakenly believe the term "Realtor" is synonymous with real estate agent. It is

not. According to the NAR's website, *the term REALTOR® is a registered collective membership mark that identifies a real estate professional who is a member of the NATIONAL ASSOCIATION of REALTORS® and subscribes to its strict* **Code of Ethics.**

The Code establishes time-honored and baseline principles that come from the collective experiences of REALTORS® since the Code of Ethics was first established in 1913. Those principles can be loosely defined as:

- *Loyalty to clients;*
- *Fiduciary (legal) duty to clients;*
- *Cooperation with competitors*
- *Truthfulness in statements and advertising*

There are many other designations and acronyms. Everything from resort specialists to working with senior citizens. If there is a niche market, it's safe to say there is probably a professional certification with a fancy acronym!

While agents *without* designations can be as superb as those *with* the designation, one thing you know that you are getting with an agent who has additional designations is a commitment to excellence and professional growth.

9. Do ask friends for referrals

Getting recommendations from friends is an essential step in finding a great real estate agent. But when asking, **be very specific.** This is where most people go wrong in seeking referrals. Be extremely specific about what you are looking for in an agent!

A simple question like, "Do you know any good agents?" won't cut it.

What your friends and family like in a real estate agent *may not be what you like*. To evaluate a recommendation, ask your friend or relative a few additional questions:

- What about this agent do you like?
- What was your experience working with this agent?
- What didn't you like about this agent?
- What do you wish they had done differently?

If you like what you hear, jump on the real estate agents' website and find out as much as you can about them. Feel free to visit them at an open house.

We Rise
By Lifting
Others Up.

And again, I think it's extremely important for a real estate agent to have a public list of testimonials available. Testimonials are the only way of proving that past clients are *happy* clients. If they weren't, they wouldn't have agreed to do a testimonial! Some testimonials from my clients can be found at www.sellyourhomequigley.com

10. *Do* choose an agent who responds to communication

How soon did she return your call? Did she return your call at all? Does she respond to text messages, emails, social media, or blog comments? For how long? This may seem minor, but how soon and how often an agent responds to your communication will tell you a lot about who she is and how she works.

Keep in mind that some agents will put their best foot forward when first meeting, so first impressions may be deceptive. Ask for some references, and then follow up with them to see what they thought about the agent's responsiveness.

Personally, I guarantee all of my clients that I will stay in touch with them *at least* once a week! (Usually it's a lot more than once per week!).

One more thing—remember that YOU are in the driver's seat. YOU are in control. YOU are buying or selling a house... ...not the real estate agent. Don't let the real estate agent's agenda get in front of yours.

I met a woman who I will call "Mary" (not her real name). Mary grew up on a farm in southern Wilmington, and was a country girl at heart. The home she was raised in was an old 2-story home, with lots of character. The yard had many mature trees and a long winding driveway. *That's* what she wanted.

Unfortunately, her real estate agent was only showing her ramblers in town....and kept making strange comments like, "As we age we should make sure to have a main floor bedroom and a smaller yard." In fact, "Maybe you should just rent," the real estate agent told her.

Well, wouldn't you know it... ...it just so happened that this agent owned a rental property in town and badly needed a new tenant!

Mary was so discouraged and frustrated that she almost fell for it. Eventually, she found an agent who listened to her and what her dream was. Mary didn't care about a main floor bedroom. She could deal with that. Mary was also very independent and was very capable of handling a large yard and long driveway.

Moral of the story? Don't settle for someone else's idea of perfect for you. It's YOUR money. It's YOUR home. Follow YOUR dream!

GOOD THINGS
COME TO THOSE
WHO WAIT...EXCEPT
WHEN IT COMES TO
PUTTING IN AN OFFER

5

First-Time Homebuyer? Six Things You MUST Do (That Most First-Time Homebuyers Completely Ignore)

"Owning a home is the keystone of wealth...both financial affluence and emotional security" - Suze Orman

Buying your first house can be scary.

It's a huge investment – quite possibly the biggest one you will ever make in your lifetime. And unless you grew up with parents who were real estate agents, you are probably a little intimidated by the whole process. Heck, my kids are growing up with a mom and dad, both, who are real estate agents and even *they* will be intimidated!

How do you know if you are buying the right house?

Who do you trust?

What do you need to know about your credit score?

When should you get pre-approved?

How much can you afford?

These are the kinds of questions that are probably racing through your mind right now. Hopefully my book (and specifically this chapter) will help you navigate these unchartered waters.... making your first home-buying experience pleasant and memorable.

And keep this in mind throughout the process: **it will be worth it to be a homeowner!**

1. Check Your Credit Score

Let's start from the top. You aren't going to be able to buy a home unless you have at least *pretty good* credit. It doesn't have to be perfect, but it can't be below average or mediocre. So, now is the time to clean it up before you start the home buying process!

What you *don't* want are a bunch of surprises showing up on your score down the road when you are ready to close on a house. This is a *badddddd* time to find out that your credit isn't what you thought it was! I've had homebuyers cry on my shoulder (literally) when they found out their credit score prevented them from buying a home.

It's better to take care of this right away so you don't have to worry about it when you actually start house hunting—even if you are absolutely certain your score is good. You never know what could be on it.

You can get a copy of your credit score from the three major credit agencies (or by talking to a local bank):

- Experian
- Equifax
- TransUnion

2. Evaluate Your Credit Cards

When it comes to credit cards, you need to think wisely about how you are using them. Many, many, many people abuse their "plastic." Having bad habits with credit cards WILL prevent you from someday buying your first house. That's a fact.

Let that sink in!

This specifically haunts first time homebuyers, because they usually have a relatively low income. Because their expenses take up a larger chunk of that income, any additional credit card debt makes it difficult for a bank to justify loaning them money. They have a thin "margin" every month, and that scares potential lenders.

Typically, banks don't want you to spend anymore than 30% of your monthly income directly on housing. For example, if you're making $2,000/month, that equates to $600. When you add credit card debt (which usually has VERY HIGH interest rates) to the equation, banks will *not* approve your mortgage.

I'm not saying you can't have *some* credit card debt—it completely depends on your various income/expenses/debt ratios. **Preferably you have zero debt, and you pay your credit card balance in full every single month.** But remember: the worst type of debt to have is high interest rate credit card debt (which was probably used to buy unnecessary consumer goods like TV's, clothes, spring break vacations, etc).

So the next time your friends are headed to the City of Chicago, a Cubs game, or going to see a movie on opening night.....stay at home. It will feel weird at first, but you will soon get addicted to the emotional rush of saving money. As you pay down any debt you may have, you are one step closer to a better credit score......and your first home!

There *are* amazing "first time homebuyer" mortgage programs out there, but you need to have solid finances!

So before you even start *looking* at homes, get strategic about this. Read a Dave Ramsey book or two, and apply his advice. If you have outstanding credit card balances, pay them down to zero! Live extremely frugally, and make temporary lifestyle sacrifices.

Trust me—it will feel amazing when you have little to no credit card debt, and you're able to qualify for a home because of your above average credit score!

3. Create a Budget

Before you ever buy a house you should create a monthly budget based upon what you would pay *if you already owned a house.*

This exercise has a number of advantages. First, it teaches you to live within your housing budget when it isn't as risky to do so. Living for three or four months on a "restricted" budget will give you an idea of whether or not your expectations are realistic.

In other words, it will teach you what you can truly afford. Better to find out when you have the income than when you already have the house.....but don't have the money.

In my experience, many first time homebuyers buy a house that's at the top of their budget. They technically can afford it, but they have little to no money left over every month for entertainment, eating out, etc. It's no fun to live in your own home if you can't go to the movies once a month, eat out with your friends, etc.

Plan accordingly!

In addition, you'll be able to save more money toward a potential down payment (which you should have been building for a number of years by now), pay off any remaining debt (like credit cards or car loans), save money for any moving expenses, and build an emergency fund.

And if you don't already have a few thousand dollars in an emergency fund, you really shouldn't buy a house. Things *will* go wrong. A furnace could go out (not a fun thing during Illinois winters), air conditioning could stop working, water leaks in the ceiling, siding repaired, or your car could break down.

You NEED to have some liquid cash available to pay for unforeseen "emergency" expenses.

The goal of this exercise is to pay above anything that you pay as a renter. So on top of your normal housing bills, start to pay an additional amount based upon items like:

- Home mortgage
- Mortgage insurance
- Annual property taxes
- HOA (home owner association) fees
- Home furnishings

- Maintenance and repairs (even if you are moving into a new house, expect something to break down....because it will!)
- Cleaning
- Utilities

If you're currently renting, ask your landlord for all of the fees that he pays, and include those in your monthly budget. This budget is useful, too, when it actually comes time to make an offer on a home – you can present this budget to your lender for additional evidence that you can afford the loan since mortgage lenders like to see bank and credit card statements. Plus, it will give the bank confidence that you are a financially responsible adult that knows how to plan and budget.

Another thing to consider is special circumstances with your insurance policy. **Contact your insurance agent**

Oh, and this is a great time to start collecting pay stubs and all financial statements in a folder that you will keep current as new information comes through the door!

4. Find a Lender AND GET PREAPPROVED

Next to your real estate agent, the mortgage lender is the other most important professional you'll want to meet when it comes to buying a new home. A good real estate agent can introduce you to a good lender. I know several great ones! Please feel free to contact me for their names, reviews, and contact information.

How do you spot a good lender? Make sure you interview several candidates, check references, and **don't allow anyone to run your credit score until you've picked a lender.** If several people try to access your score over a short period of time, your credit score can suffer.

By the way, avoid choosing a lender based on "points" (especially if we are talking about just a quarter or two of points). In fact, you might be tempted to work with an online lender because of low interest rates. DON'T. Online lenders – and their underwriters – are usually hard to contact and are not in control of the situation.

You'll just have to trust me on this one—I would much rather work with a lender that is a great communicator, is trustworthy, and is responsive to my needs than a lender who is none of those things... ...but offers a much lower interest rate.

If you're a first time homebuyer, the interest rate doesn't matter that much anyways—a difference of half a percent or even a full percent on a $100,000 home won't make that much of a difference on your monthly payment.

You're much better off choosing a lender based on quality of service and personality than you are by "whoever is the cheapest."

Here's the most important thing: get pre-approved, *especially* if you are in a competitive seller's market (meaning there is a surplus of buyers, not homes). At the time I'm writing this book in, we are in a buyer's market....but that can and will change!

A good lender will help you understand all of your financing options (caps on certain types of financing), in addition to the pros and cons of each option.

This process will also help you align your budget (the one that you've been working on for the past four months, right?), and give you a practical idea of what you can and cannot afford.

A good lender is almost like a personal finance consultant. They won't just quote you the latest interest rate—they'll guide you through the process to make sure you understand your options and make an informed decision on your mortgage. If your mortgage lender does *not* do this, find a new lender!

Once you've chosen a lender, sit down with them and have them walk you through your credit report.

5. Find a Real Estate Agent

A (good) real estate agent serves a very unique role: *objectivity*. Think of the agent as that little angel sitting on your shoulder asking if that house with the infinity pool is really within your budget.

Of course, a good agent will guide you through the buying process. She can show you homes in neighborhoods that fit your requirements....and she should know the market and lead you to new listings before they even get on the market!

Compete With Others,
Become Bitter.

Compete With Yourself,
Become BETTER.

As you probably did yourself, **most home buyers start their search online**—but eventually, you'll more than likely work with an agent you know through a recommendation from family and friends.

It pays to *ask early* for recommendations and interview them early in the process. Even if you are six to nine months out from buying, finding a good agent can take a long time, so the sooner you look, the better.

This means if you are planning on buying a home in September, you should be looking for an agent as early as January. Don't wait until the last minute.

I've written extensively in this book about how to choose the *right* real estate agent. Make sure you read it cover to cover!

6. Be Ready

Once you've evaluated your credit score, worked on a new budget, contacted a real estate agent, and found a lender, it's *now* time to start looking at houses.

Unfortunately, most first time homebuyers do NONE of these things.

They immediately go online and start looking for homes. Some even start driving around to check out properties they found online. This is a HUGE mistake, because you have absolutely no idea what you qualify for, what you can afford, etc.

Hopefully this chapter convinces you to "take care of business" *before* you actually start house hunting!

If you are in a seller's market, you'll now understand why I recommend that you do everything above *first*: you must be ready to pounce on a great house when you find it. In hot markets, every day matters. Heck, sometimes every *hour* matters.

If you don't have your down payment, budget, and pre-approval, you might miss out on the perfect home.

And it's important during this time (it could take anywhere from three to six months) to keep your financial record *clean*. Don't make any major purchases, and keep on top of your bills. **The biggest mistake I've seen is buying a car within a year of buying a house.** Unless your income has gone up significantly since you financed your car, it will be very difficult to qualify for a mortgage if you already have monthly car payment obligations. So if you're driving a nicer, newer car, ask yourself if you'd rather have *that*, or own a home. Chances are you'd be better off driving a reliable used car, and putting the difference towards your dream of owning a home.

So, again, don't make any major purchases before applying for mortgage pre-approval. You don't want that final look at your finances to be disrupted.

And before you actually make an offer on a house, do the following:

- Call the utility providers (electric, water, sewer, garbage) to find out average monthly billing
- Find out about any potential homeowner association fees
- Look at the property taxes

Now, add all of those extra expenses to your budget, and ask yourself an honest question: **can you *still* afford the house?**

Here's the bottom line: don't fall for a beautiful home if the expenses are going to drive you over your budget. Don't let anyone push you to go into the upper ends of your budget...or over your budget. Even if you could technically afford the house, if you don't have any money left over, you are not going to be able to take care of the house!

Also avoid spending all your available cash on the down payment and closing costs. Otherwise, if you run into emergency repairs and unexpected costs, you will have to ask your parents, friends, or other family to bail you out... ....because the bank will not.

#HOMEBUYERTIPS

THE SELLER PAYS AGENT
COMMISSIONS, THERE IS
NO COST TO YOU TO
USE A REAL ESTATE
AGENT TO PROTECT
YOU DURING THE
BIGGEST TRANSACTION
IN YOUR LIFE.

Should You Sell Your Home Without An Agent? Insider Tips For Marketing Your Home As A "For Sale By Owner"

"Stop Selling. Start Helping" – Zig Ziglar

The easiest way to teach is through stories. Here's a *true* story that I will never forget.....

     "Cheryl" had a home on a local lake here in Will County (Cheryl is not her real name). She had a *for sale by owner* sign in her yard. I introduced myself and asked if I could help her. She literally chased me off the property, saying "real estate agents are thieves," and that she was selling it herself.

I guess everyone is entitled to their opinion, so I left her alone.

It took about 2 days before I drove by again.....and saw a moving truck!

"Good for her," I thought to myself, "she must have gotten lucky and found the perfect buyer."

I knew Cheryl's neighbor (which is how I originally found out about the property), so I stopped in to speak with her. She said that she had in fact sold the house. Now, I knew that this house *should have* sold for around $260,000 at that time. Usually FSBO listings don't get full market value, so I was guessing she had accepted a lowball offer to get such a quick sale. Maybe $220k or $230k.

I was wrong.

She sold it, all by herself, for.....**$128,000!!!** I wish I was kidding. I'm not making this story up! Think of how long it would take to save up the difference between what her home was actually worth and what she sold it for. She flushed a lifetime of savings down the toilet. What a tragedy. I suppose she avoided capital gains taxes, if that's any consolation.

Now, obviously this is an extreme (yet true) example of what can happen when you try to do it "on your own." Not everyone will make a mistake this costly. But you should be aware of the risks!

For sale by owners have a reputation in our industry. Amongst real estate agents, we even have a slang term for them: "FSBO's," pronounced *fizzbo's*.

As in the "fizz" created by soda pop, and "bows" used to fire arrows.

Fizzbo's.

Anyways, there are typically two main reasons homeowners decide to sell their home **without** using a licensed real estate agent.

1. They want to save $ on the commission because they feel they can do it themselves (cut out the middleman)

2. They originally listed their home with a licensed real estate agent, but are disappointed with the agent's mediocre performance/marketing plan.

Here's what you should know: over 90% of FSBO's eventually list with a licensed real estate agent. It's almost inevitable.

Why?

Sellers soon realize that selling a $200,000 product (or whatever price the home is listed at) is not as easy as pounding a sign into the yard and waiting for the phone to ring. And even in hot markets where that can work, it's almost a full time job responding to the phone calls, requests for tours, etc. If the seller has a fulltime job or other time commitments, this makes things *extremely* difficult.

And in our modern age, I think a major reason that many homeowners try to "cut out the middleman" and avoid using a real estate agent can be summed up in one phrase: **the Internet.**

People mistakenly believe that homes are commodities. They think to themselves, "I'll just take a few pictures, write a paragraph or two about the features, upload it to a local *For Sale By Owner* website, and wait for the phone to ring!"

And then they wait.

And wait.

And wait.

The phone never rings. If it does, potential buyers are usually looking to score a great deal. They throw out lowball offers. And I can't blame them.

Here's why: when your home is listed as a "For Sale By Owner," *the buyer knows that there isn't a middleman.*

They feel that *they* are entitled to some of that extra profit—not you, the seller. So typically they make lower offers than they otherwise would. This practically eliminates any hypothetical "savings" that may have been realized............if the home is lucky enough to attract any offers to begin with. In fact, many homes listed without an agent fail to attract a single offer or phone call.

When this inevitably happens, the seller gets frustrated. *Very* frustrated (and understandably so).

Eventually, months later, he or she will end up listing the house with a licensed agent.

I won't beat around the bush here—I firmly believe it is in your best interest to buy and sell real estate with an experienced, licensed agent (preferably a certified Realtor).

But............

If you're dead set on selling your home *without* a real estate agent, I want to share some insider secrets with you. It's super easy—just go online to a special website created for all the *For Sale By Owner* listings:

http://www.forsalebyowner.com/

Quigley Sell Your Home

Once you've logged on to the website, you will find lots of helpful information that will come in handy if you decide to sell your home without an agent. Again, while I don't recommend it, I *do* want you to be successful.

I've been around real estate in Will and Cook County for over 12 years now—I have been around Real Estate for most of my adult life, and before getting my license. This is my world and what I am surrounded with daily and have been for years.

As a licensed agent, I have successfully done many transactions (many of them were homes that were listed with me because they originally failed to sell as a *FSBO*).

When it comes to real estate, mistakes can be really expensive. I want you to sit down and truly think about whether or not selling your own home would benefit you, or whether listing with an agent is best. This ultimately is your choice.

BONUS CHAPTER

Think Your House Is Ready For The Market? Here's Why "Staging" Will Help Your Home Sell Faster....... For A Higher Price!

"Buyers only know what they see. Not the way its going to be" - Barb Schwarz

Time and money...... two things most of us wish we had *more* of, right?

Work and stress, two things most of us wish we had *less* of, right?

When it comes to selling a house, these realities may become foremost in our minds. If there was ever a time you needed professional expertise to help you through a process.....this is it.

A Realtor who is knowledgeable in the market, knows what is selling and for how much, **and** knows how to look at the house with "buyers eyes," and see exactly what should be done *before* listing, can save you time, money, work and stress.

After writing the listing agreement, a competent Realtor will advertise your property, schedule showings with your approval, provide the necessary forms, represent you in negotiating a contract for purchase, show you what your expected net proceeds will be, keep you constantly informed of all activity on your property, and can arrange for closing services.

If time is an issue (as it should be, after all time is money), **getting a house ready for market is crucial.** Grab those first lookers, because they knew enough about the property to be interested in scheduling a showing! They most likely have seen it online (about 90% of buyers shop online first). They liked the photos, know the square footage, room layout, etc....so when they step into the door, make sure they know this is the house they've been looking for! It should be appealing and welcoming.

A Realtor needs to know how to make a house appeal to the senses. Most sellers need help in reaching that point and *most* Realtors (not all) don't know or don't want to risk offending clients and losing the listing.........so they are reluctant to offer staging advice.

One of my very first listings resulted from a seller who called me after his 6 month listing expired with another agency, telling me he had asked the listing agent, "What can we do to help our house show better?"

The other agent had told him the house was fine! I could, however, see a lot of room for improvement. I was able to give him a very do-able list that he and his wife promptly dug into, spending less than $500 total. It resulted in a sale to the very next buyers who were shown the house. They were thrilled and remarked, "I wish we had called you 6 months ago!"

Of course, not all staging projects will be that inexpensive. In fact, the national average spent on staging a house is about 1-3% of the list price. How well the house has been maintained is a huge factor, if the roof or basement leaks, those types of issues obviously are a higher priority than painting and redecorating.

It is important to remember that *staging is not covering up problems!*

Often, Realtors will provide the seller with a beginning list price and ask them to consider a price reduction if there are no offers within 30 days. This price reduction can be substantial **and unnecessary** if part of that money is spent up front on presenting the property at its best and making sure that the original price is on target and not unrealistically bumped up to impress the sellers and secure the listing.

Staging Statistics

The National Association of Realtors states that those who generally spend 1-3% of the value of their home preparing their home to sell (staging), reap 8-10% in average price value (fewer price reductions, carrying costs, or home sitting on the market). Wow!

Your Home's "Staging Potential" at 1%:_____= 8%_____in Average Price Value

This formula shows that using *conservative* figures, if your home is worth $500,000 and you spend 1% to stage it - $5000 (this figure includes much more than staging fees, this includes new furniture, paying electricians, painters, and carpenters if needed)....you will then expect an 8% return on your investment. Which is $40,000!

Statistics show that staging your home for sale will shorten your "Days on Market" and bring you a higher price for your home. Period.

BUYERS?

What about buyers? As important as it is for Realtors and their sellers to know about proper staging, it is equally important for a Realtor to know what problems or potential problems to look for in a house when helping prospective buyers.

As emphasized elsewhere in this book, a buyer's agent will make sure that there is a home inspection contingency included in a purchase agreement, have knowledge and experience in home construction and maintenance, *and* be well equipped to negotiate with the sellers' agent after any issues are discovered during the home inspection.

An ethical and experienced Realtor will know when to advise their buyers to walk away from the home they *thought* they wanted, even though it might mean more work for the Realtor to get the sale and commission check they are hoping for!

By Randi Lynn Kalinski-Quigley
Licensed Broker/Realtor
MLS 705823
Coldwell Banker Realty
SellYourHomeQuigley@gmail.com
708.446.0328

ABOUT ME

"Go The Extra Mile, It's Never Ever Crowded" – Randi Lynn

First off, Thank You So Much for reading my book. I just wanted to write a little bit more about myself so that you could get to know me a better.

I was born at Palos Hospital in June of 1983. I primarily grew up in Cook County, though I did move a lot growing up. I attended Central Middle School in Tinley Park and then went to Carl Sandburg High School, graduated class of 2001.

I grew up with my parents, and 2 sisters to who I am very close with these days... My parents separated when I was in Grade School and because of that, I have always learned that I wanted to be able to become a strong, successful business owner. I was forced to grow up pretty fast. Being that my parents were separated, both had to work full time in order to provide for our family.

I saw how hard it was to work full time and still have designated family time. I was a cheerleader growing up. Took Ice Skating lessons as well... I always truly believed that this world had so much potential to be such an amazing place! I realized early on that in order to get where you wanted to be in life, you truly needed to believe in yourself.

"The Power Of Positive" is what I like to call it. Think Positive, Train your mind to see the positive in every situation.

I graduated early from High School and immediately went into working Full Time with my mom's Staffing Business, while attending a few classes at Moraine Valley just getting some of my general education classes out of the way. I learned quickly the art of sales. Though at that time, I hadn't quite figured out exactly what I wanted to do for a living.

About a year later, I decided to pursue Interior Design. I have always loved houses and decorating, thought about Real Estate but loved the idea of using my creativity to shine! I obtained my Associates in Interior Design and after talking to the Schools about what Designers were making right out of college, it scared me. I had to pay for my own education so I had to make sure that I would be able to do so with the career choice that I made.

So making a Business Decision, as I now like to call it, I transferred to Saint Xavier to where I then pursued my degree in Business Administration, Double Majoring in Marketing and Finance. I graduated and somehow found my way into Accounting. I was working for an amazing organization called SOS Childrens Villages. I started pursuing my Masters in Accounting.

After deciding to start a family, I resigned from my position to become a stay at home mommy. I have now 4 beautiful children and I am completely blessed to have all I do.

But very shortly after being home with them (at that time it was 2) I had learned that I began to slowly lose myself. I opened up my own Marketing Business, with a product at that time I truly believed in, and was very successful. I felt alive and realized quickly that my calling was Marketing and Working with People. Now, real estate has always been something that intrigued me. Especially with my background in Marketing and Interior Design.

I have been surrounded by Real Estate now Each and EVERY SINGLE DAY of My Life since I have been 20 years old and it has taught me so much.

I am so beyond grateful that I decided to pursue my dreams and become a Realtor. This, by far, has been one of the best decisions I have ever made in my entire life. I absolutely love what I do. I love helping people with their "American Dream" and I truly feel I am compassionate towards my clients. This is a Very Big time in your life and one that should not be taken lightly. It is my job as a Realtor to make sure that I am there with my clients through every step of the way. To help with questions and be there to make this process as enjoyable and exciting as it should be.

I am truly humbled by all that I have learned and I am so excited to see what the future holds. I would love the opportunity to meet with you and see if we could be a great fit and I thank you again for taking the time out to read my book.

I have found my true calling in life and success, to me, is truly making a difference in others' lives. I believe that's what I am able to do, with being a Realtor.

AWARDS

I have been a real estate broker now full time since 2013, earning many awards from Centurion, International Diamond Society Award, Quality Service Customer Service Awards, and hold designations including SRES (Seniors Real Estate Specialist) and Certified Corporate Relocation Specialist. 2014 I was honored as in the Top 10 Agents of my entire Region and I am currently the Top Selling Agent at Coldwell Banker's Orland Park Office; Selling an average of 14 million to 22 million plus per year. My husband, Steve, joined Real Estate in 2018 and with his rural background as a Full Time Farmer, his expertise in these properties is undeniable. Together we provide service that stands above all the rest. We live the life of Real Estate and this has become more than just a career. It is our passion and true calling. Living the lifestyle and always putting our clients best interests at heart. Treating you as part of our family is how we run our business.

"Every great dream begins with a dreamer. Always remember, you have within you the strength, the patience, and the passion to reach for the stars to change the world."

Harriet Tubman

CREDITS

Photography by:

© **CINDY GAMBOA + SUSAN MELLENS, INTERIOR INSIGHT**

Printed in the United States
by Baker & Taylor Publisher Services